Frantz Fanon for the 21st Century Volume 1

Frantz Fanon's Discourse of Racism and Culture, the Negro and the Arab Deconstructed

Daurius Figueira

Table of Contents

This book is dedicated to Steve Biko whose murder (September 12, 1977) was necessary to the success of the project to create the post-apartheid neo-colonial South African State. For Biko my tears cannot cease to flow! "The most potent weapon in the hands of the oppressor is the mind of the oppressed." Steve Biko.

Introduction

This is a deconstruction of Frantz Fanon's work "Black Skin, White Masks" which was published first in French as "Peau Noire. Masques Blancs" in 1952 with the intention to present the potency of Fanon's analysis of racism and culture in the North Atlantic for the 21st century. We are in the second decade of the twenty first century and in the North Atlantic there is a public reappearance of the spectrum of expressions embraced by white racist discourse: from white supremacy, to fascism, to National Socialism, white nationalism and white supremacist imperialism are all now in the public political space challenging the post-world war hegemony of white liberal racism thereby forcing this hegemonic form to reformulate itself in a quest to retain hegemony. This is a North Atlantic reality now expressed that was never supposed to exist and to become an event of note as it is now mainstream politics. To explain this white racist reality is compulsory for all non-white races on this planet for this 21st century North Atlantic reality poses a grave threat to us all whether we live in the North Atlantic or not. But the crux of the matter is the tools we use to strip bare this reality, to expose its nakedness to us, to facilitate understanding, for it is not only futile and stupid to use the tools of white racist discourse to analyse itself, it is downright dangerous for we can end up totally disarmed and brain dead until such time that we face personal death at the hands of those intent on purging the threat we pose to "their" world. This is why we are compelled to turn critically to the works of Frantz Fanon for Fanon's contribution to the ferment, agitation, the quest for change and Revolution in the 1950s, 1960s, 1970s and thereafter in the Third World and the North Atlantic speaks for itself and demands that its relevance for the 21st century be established.

The methodology utilised in the analysis of Fanon's discourse of racism and culture, the Negro and the Arab as presented in "Black Skin, White Masks" and selections from his articles of the same time period collected and published in English after his death as "Toward the African Revolution" is deconstruction. The text is read to uncover the core discursive concepts of the discourse then every core concept is articulated to the limits of its meanings to uncover the ideas, worldview and power relations contained therein. Finally, all such core concepts are presented in their order of appearance in the text to map out the structure, content, strategic intent, power relations and operational mechanisms of the discourse/power. By this process Fanon's discourse is laid bare, stripped naked revealing the potency of its analytical insights of the discourse of white racist supremacy, the power relations of the discourse of white racist supremacy and those constituted by white power namely the Negro and the Arab. In turn weaknesses, failings, the continued use of white racist ideas and its impact on Fanon's discourse and personal characteristics are also revealed which informs the process of review for application across time/space,

in this instance the 21st century. Throughout the text the key concepts are identified and analysed along with the overriding reality for they are part of a discourse that Fanon formulated and unleashed.

In keeping with deconstruction methodology all terms utilised by Fanon in his text are repeated in my textual analysis, even if I have rejected specific terminology utilised by Fanon. This is expressively so with reference to Fanon's use of the white man's invention 'Negro' to describe persons of the African Diaspora of the West specifically. Negro in and for itself illustrates the use of language and discourse to assault those strategically targeted for domination through the use of racism as an instrument of power. Fanon himself deals with the problematic of the use of black as a descriptor of a specific type of non-white persons otherwise known as Negroes. But the dynamic of the black/white duality results in white defining and conjuring black as a soul which is draped over specific non-white peoples. Black then expresses subservience to white, its genesis through white power and to describe ourselves as black relentlessly affirms our domination by white power for there is no black specificity without white definition. This can never be the path to Liberation for this path must be expressed via self-definition that is independent where we define ourselves for our benefit not by those seeking to dominate us.

In this entire process of deconstruction, I make no claim to North Atlantic mythic objectivity for I am also being deconstructed as I am the product of a racist social order and racism has impacted my perception of self, my growth and development and my life chances and opportunities. From my first reading of Fanon in the 1970s his works continue to impact my being as I recall and reflect upon painful memories of racist assaults on my being from a tender age to adulthood. Racism especially when it is unleashed upon you by those you are told is your blood relative and you form an expectation of behaviour from them and they destroy that expectation with a racist assault changes your outlook on life forever and if you don't intervene on your behalf you will become a cold hard hearted racist consumed with self-hate which is the extreme type. You will then find instances of my pain expressed in the text, just instances as I reserve the full description for my story. For I am Miscegenated born of a white father and a mixed non-white mother and therein lies my event horizon for racism hurts!

Chapter 1
The Psychoexistential Complex of the White/Non-White Races

Black-white relation/complex, Aberrations of Effect

Fanon states in the Introduction of the book: "Why write this book? No one has asked me for it. Especially those to whom it is directed. Well? Well, I reply quite calmly that there are too many idiots in this world. And having said it, I have the burden of proving it" (Fanon 1977 pg. 7). Fanon wrote the book to debunk the idiots in the world but what is the topic of the book which involves debunking the idiots? Fanon states his position as follows: "What does a man want? What does the black man want?" (Fanon 1977 pg. 8). Fanon is then dealing with the existential issues of man but specifically the "black man". Fanon continues: "At the risk of arousing the resentment of my coloured brothers, I will say that the black is not a man."" (Fanon 1977 pg. 8). Fanon is writing a book the subject of which includes himself as he is a black man and Fanon insists that he is not a man. Fanon states: "There is a zone of nonbeing, an extraordinarily sterile and arid region, an utterly naked declivity where an authentic upheaval can be born. In most cases, the black man lacks the advantage of being able to accomplish this descent into a real hell." (Fanon 1977 pg. 8). To be human for Fanon is to be able to descend into the real hell, this declivity which enables and fosters authentic upheaval, dynamism and change. The black man is denied the ability to access this real hell, the totally naked declivity which denies the black man the condition of being human. Fanon continues: "The black is a black man; that is, as the result of a series of aberrations of affect, he is rooted at the core of a universe from which he must be extricated. The problem is important. I propose nothing short of the liberation of the man of colour from himself. We shall go very slowly, there are two camps: the white and the black." (Fanon 1977 pg. 8). This black man who is denied access to the means to generate upheaval is the product of a series of aberrations of affect, he is the constituted product of a power relation where "black" is affixed to his being which locates her/him in a specific, manufactured universe which traps them in their blackness where blackness is expressed and summed up by the inability to descend into the real hell where genuine, real upheavals are created and launched from. The black humans are products of power affects which constitute a being with a black soul attached driven by an operational duality of power where white constitutes black in a bid to ensure the hegemony of white over black accomplished by the docility of black. The impact of this power relation constitutes black humans who are the results of aberrations of affect as they are simply the artifice and product of white power. Fanon's summation is that the black man must be liberated from himself as himself is the product of white power designed to serve white power through problematizing the black self. The black self has to stripped away and replaced with an alternate self that is the product of power that stands in opposition to white power but it cannot be black power as black begets white and black insists that white is understood in the dance of the duality for in this duality there is no black without white and vice versa. For the two camps are inseparable and joined at the hips via white hegemony. Black liberation then problematizes the concept of black power in contention with white power for hegemony for white begets black. The core of Fanon's discourse is then the duality of white and black, its power relations and the impact of these power relations on the personalities of the white and black races. Fanon continues: "To us, the man who adores the Negro is as "sick" as the man who abominates him. Conversely, the black man who wants to turn his race white is as miserable as he who preaches hatred for the whites. The black man wants to be white. The white man slaves to reach a human level" (Fanon 1977 pgs. 8-9). Fanon throws light in the introduction to the book on the complex duality that is white/black power relations and the human actors constituted by this duality where these actors project "onto the world an antinomy that coexists with him." (Fanon 1977 pg. 8). This antinomy traps both white and black into a universe driven by disharmonies that distort transcendence hence ultimately consciousness. The basis of these disharmonies, the distortion of transcendence and the encapsulation of consciousness is race hate expressed via racist discourse. This is the nature of the universe where the black man is rooted and from which he must be liberated, the domain of the aberrations of affect.

Dual Narcissism, Anomalies of Affect

Fanon defines his task as follows: "In the course of this essay we shall observe the development of an effort to understand the black-white relation. The white man is sealed in his whiteness. The black man in his blackness. We shall seek to ascertain the direction of this dual narcissism and the motivations that inspire it. Concern with the elimination of a vicious circle has been the only guideline for my efforts. There is a fact: White men consider themselves superior to black men. There is another fact: Black men want to prove to white men, at all costs the richness of their thought, the equal value of their intellect. How do we extricate ourselves?" (Fanon 1977 pgs. 8-10). Fanon's book is then the expression of an effort to deconstruct this black-white relation. As a relation it has a dynamic and impact but it also has power relations and psychological reality. Fanon insists that its dynamic is driven by dual narcissism as black and white are directly irreconcilably different divided by a chasm of whiteness vs blackness. But this dual narcissism is tempered, even limited by the duality of the superior/inferior complexes exhibited by the white and black man respectively. The dual narcissism can then only be operationally active and exist within the space created by the white-black relation where it shares space with the superiority/inferiority complex spectrum. There is then a duality of relational affects arising from the white-black dual relation which is the dual narcissism/superiority - inferiority complex relation which constitutes the "aberrations of affect" that impact white and black individuals trapped in the white-black relation. Fanon continues on his task in the book: "Indeed, I believe that only a psychoanalytical interpretation of the black problem can lay bare the anomalies of affect that are responsible for the structure of the complex." (Fanon 1977 pg. 10). Fanon's task is then a psychoanalytical deconstruction of the black problem but his key to this deconstruction is the revealing of the structure of the complex that impacts the white-black relation which is the product of the operational activity of the aberrations/ anomalies of affect. The black problem is the product of the operational activity of the aberrations/anomalies of affect through the structure of the complex which afflicts white and black hence the white-black relation is the white-black complex. Of the two problems, the white and black of the white-black relation/ complex Fanon has chosen to address the black problem in the book. Fanon then makes a statement that illustrates the power of the structure of the complex and by extension the anomalies/aberrations of effect as follows: "However painful it may be for me to accept this conclusion; I am obliged to state it: For the black man there is only one destiny. And it is white." (Fanon 1977 pg. 10). Fanon has already stated the basis for this conclusion in the preceding text. As long as the white-black complex operationally exists there is only one outcome for those classified as non-white, specifically black in Fanon's book is to be white with black skins hence black skins, white masks. For the strategy of the white-black complex is to subjugate all non-white peoples to the white North Atlantic race through the operation of specific typologies of inferior races that define race specific racist mechanisms of the white-non-white complex with their specific aberrations/anomalies of affect.

Psychoexistential Complex

Fanon continues with describing the nature of his project as follows: "The analysis that I am undertaking is psychological. In spite of this it is apparent to me that the effective disalienation of the black man entails an immediate recognition of social and economic realities. If there is an inferiority complex, it is the double process: -primarily, economic; -subsequently, the internalisation-or, better, the epidermalisation- of this inferiority." (Fanon 1977 pgs. 10-11). The white-black complex has a socio-economic reality that demands its formulation and sustainable operationalisation. White socio-economic dominance, hegemony over non-white peoples demands the white-non-white complexes specifically in Fanon's case presented in his book the white-black complex. In this reality race and class are then linked which necessitates that all power mechanisms must carry a white racist supremacist/ black inferiority mechanism. Fanon then insists that white economic dominance and the duality created with black economic subservience drives the internalisation of white superiority/black inferiority. But there much more than internalisation as the white-black complex brands black skin as the universal symbol of inferiority, backwardness, savagery or all states of existence that are not that of the members of the white race. The skin of the black race then is a sign to the white race of what to expect from the wearer of this skin where your skin is your sin! The wearer of black skin then becomes all that the skin symbolises, all the messages of nature, morals, values and virtues or lack thereof the skin sends. The skin is an artifice of the white race, invented by the white race, defined by the white race to serve the hegemony of the white race and when you refuse to liberate yourself from this power game you can only be white in your non-white specificity which never leaves you, creating aberrations that plague the psyche of the non-whites. Fanon describes this reality as follows: "I believe that the fact of the juxtaposition of the white and black races has created a massive psychoexistential complex. I hope by analysing it to destroy it." (Fanon 1977 pg. 12). This massive complex is psychoexistential in nature where the existential reality is coupled with the psyche, the psychology of the individuals as a duality impacting and influencing the strategic imperatives of each other. The existential domain sees the allocation of space, resources, power driven by racist supremacy/inferiority which demands an order which produces compliant individuals. The psychological is impacted even moulded by the demands of the existential, of power for compliant individuals but there are dynamisms in this realm which constantly seek expression and resistance which constantly challenge the hegemony sought and maintained. Power and power relations then drive this psychoexistential complex where the existential and the psyche are welded together in the service of power which is ever dynamic. There is then a dynamic to this psychoexistential complex where individuals and groups are constantly probing for the limits of control, hegemony which demands perpetual response and renewal. It must evolve over time and space to ensure its sustainability and the fact that it continues to survive must be explained. Fanon insists that his analysis is then the basis for the movement to destroy it what is then needed

in the 21st century is a new analysis where we commence from Fanon's analysis and move forward. Fanon continues with describing his work to follow: "I shall demonstrate elsewhere that what is often called the black soul is a white man's artifact." (Fanon 1977 pg. 14). The much vaunted black man's soul is a mass produced product manufactured by the white man formulated and attached to the black human/non-white to ensure he/she is a black human/non-white, the invention of white hegemony for the express purpose of ensuring the sustainability of white hegemony, white power. To vaunt this mechanism of white power and to define yourself by it and to proclaim your self-worth and humanity by it is in fact to affirm our inherent inferiority in the face of the inherent superiority of the white man, massa.

Black Abyss

In the closing section of the introduction to his book Fanon states: "The educated Negro, slave of the spontaneous and cosmic Negro myth, feels at a given stage that his race no longer understands him. Or that he no longer understands it." "And it is with rage in his mouth and abandon in his heart that he buries himself in the vast black abyss. We shall see that this attitude, so heroically absolute, renounces the present and the future in the name of mystical past." (Fanon 1977 pg. 14). Fanon addresses the specific condition of the "educated Negro" who is alienated from his race as she/he clings to the Negro myth. A myth formulated by racist white hegemony and operationalised through the white-black complex. A cosmic and spontaneous myth which alienates from self and the race group and leads the educated Negro into the vast black abyss the singularity produced by the white-black complex. The singularity driven by white supremacy where the black, the educated Negro has no concept of the present and future only a mystical past that ensures the sustainability of the white-black complex which serves white hegemony. All blacks trapped in the black abyss have then a flawed, sterile ontology and epistemology which betrays the reality that the knowledge bases of non-white races are constantly under assault to ensure that the knowledge, the discourses and worldviews through which we see and visualise and act upon and in the world are all the products of or subservient to white hegemonic discourse. All subservient non-white discourse then constitutes and ensures the vast black abyss is sustainable the effectiveness of which spans 1492 to 2018. This vast black abyss denies a present and a future vitally necessary to exercising white hegemony and it constitutes a mystical past which grounds those who internalise it to be repeatedly condemned to cyclical servility, inaction, self-hate and self-immolation. And we the non-white races of the world are the most potent facilitators of the vast black abyss where we condemn generations of our races to in our quest to be white even though we can never be such is the power of the negation. In the final paragraph Fanon makes it clear that the base reality informing the book is limited to the French Antilles of the Caribbean island chain specifically Martinique and Guadeloupe. Fanon states: "Since I was born in the Antilles, my observations and conclusions are valid only for the Antilles-at least concerning the black man *at home*." (Fanon 1977 pg. 14). Don't read into this book what is not under study for it is geographically defined by Fanon's biography, a study of grave importance in light of the reality that the West Indian slave plantation was the laboratory that made the signal progress in the formulation and operationalisation of white, racist, supremacist, hegemony.

Chapter 2
White Language, the Negro and The Other

Language and *The Other*

In actuality Chapter one of "Black Skin, White Masks" Fanon explains his position as follows: "I attach a specific importance to the phenomenon of language. That is why I find it necessary to begin with this subject, which should provide us with one of the elements in the coloured man's comprehension of the dimension of *the other*. For it is implicit that to speak is to exist absolutely for the other." (Fanon 1977 pg. 17). Fanon commences his analysis with his focus on language and the Negro with specific reference to language and the comprehension of the Negro of the nature, origin and structure of *the other*. Fanon continues: "The black man has two dimensions. One with his fellows, the other with the white man. A Negro behaves differently with a white man and with another Negro. That this self-division is a direct result of colonialist subjugation is beyond question." (Fanon 1977 pg. 17). In his interaction with other humans the Negro operates a dual order of interactive strategies differentiated on the basis of race where he/she interacts with the white person entirely different from that of fellow Negroes. There are then two strategies with their specific methodologies of interaction: one for whites and one for fellow Negroes. Fanon insists that this dual strategy is the product of white colonial domination of non-whites.

Language of the Coloniser and Whiteness of the Colonised

The central problem Fanon confronts in this chapter is: "The problem that we confront in this chapter is this: The Negro of the Antilles will be proportionately whiter-that is he will come closer to being a real human being-in direct ratio to his mastery of the French language." "A man who has a language consequently possesses the world expressed and implied by that language." (Fanon 1977 pg. 18). The language of the coloniser, the massa is the primary instrument for the domination of and the rendering docile of the non-white colonised. As the non-white colonised immerse themselves in the language of the white coloniser they can only become effectively whiter in outlook and worldview for the language was devised by the civilisation of the coloniser to serve the coloniser. To immerse ourselves in the language of the coloniser is then to affirm the inherent superiority of the coloniser and their civilisation and deny our humanity, affirm our inferiority and deny our language, culture and civilisation that the coloniser disrupted and destroyed. We then become the white man's other. Fanon continues: "For the moment I want to show why the Negro of the Antilles, whoever he is, has always to face the problem of language. Furthermore, I will broaden the field of this description and through the Negro of the Antilles include every colonised man."" Every colonised people-in other words, every people in whose soul an inferiority complex has been created by the death and burial of its local cultural originality-finds itself face to face with the language of the civilising nation, that is with the culture of the mother country." (Fanon 1977 pg. 18). All colonised peoples have to face the threat posed by the problem of the language of the white dominant coloniser. Where the problem of the coloniser's language is materialised via the destruction of the culture of the colonised and the drive for white culture to fill this deliberately created void via the delivery mechanism of the coloniser's language acting in concert with the inferiority complex that white dominance breeds and enmeshes the soul of the dominated with to enable the process of whitening. Fanon states: "The colonised is elevated above his jungle status in proportion to his adoption of the mother country's cultural standards. He becomes whiter as he renounces his blackness, his jungle." (Fanon 1977 pg. 18). In a bid to fill the void created by assault on the culture and language of the colonised driven by the inferiority complex which insists that all associated with the white coloniser is superior and inherently desirable the colonised goes at the absorption of the coloniser's language and culture with gusto. In doing so she/he can only become whiter through denouncing his non-white origin which deepens and entrenches the inferiority complex of the colonised. Embracing and entrenching the culture and language of the coloniser cannot reward the colonised with liberation what it does is intensify the imprisonment of the non-white in a white artifice: the black soul. This then is the dynamic of dual narcissism that afflicts the colonised/coloniser. This reality is rooted in language, the discourse that language allows to be formulated and released. Fanon continues: "The black man who has lived in

France for a length of time returns radically changed. To express it in genetic terms, his phenotype undergoes a definitive, an absolute mutation." (Fanon 1977 pg. 19) again "For the Negro knows that over there in France there is a stereotype of him that will fasten on to him at the pier at Le Havre or Marseille." (Fanon 1977 pg. 19). Phenotypically the black man evolves into a white man in terms of worldview and the manipulation of cultural symbols including ideas and most of all language. But this is not being white for genetically the black/non-white human can never be white, in spite of the chemical and surgical alterations of the non-white body we remain trapped in our non-white destiny which drives self-hate which is expressed as self-immolation within an orbit of dual narcissism which ensures our continued domination. We are then condemned to intense acts of futility in the face of a multiple pronged assault on our non-white beings as the stereotype of the periphery is distinctly different from that of the metropole.

The Hierarchy of Blacks and Inferiority Complexes

In the course of this chapter of the book Fanon insists that the Negro of the Antilles has a specific position on European languages. He states as follows: "On the basis of other studies and my own personal observations, I want to try to show why the Negro adopts such a position, peculiar to him, with respect to the European languages. Let me point out once more that the conclusions I have reached pertain to the French Antilles; at the same time, I am not unaware that the same behaviour patterns obtain in every race that has been subjected to colonisation." (Fanon 1977 pg. 25). Fanon insists that all colonised races attach special emphasis to the task of becoming versed in the use and manipulation of the language of their coloniser. But based on his personal observations and the literature he has read he insists that the approach of the Antillean Negro to this task stands above the rest in its being unique to the Antillean Negro. Fanon continues: "I have known-and unfortunately I still know-people born in Dahomey or the Congo who pretend to be natives of the Antilles; I have known, and I still know, Antilles Negroes who are annoyed when they are suspected of being Senegalese. This is because the Antilles negro is more "civilised" than the African, that is, he is closer to the white man;" (Fanon 1977 pg. 26). Fanon insists that there is a hierarchy of colonised blacks/Negroes premised upon the exhibition of the traits of the white man, of whiteness and language is a key indicator of the degree of whiteness, of being civilised exhibited by the black/Negro and all non-whites. And the Antillean Negro is placed in a higher slot in the hierarchy vis-a-vis the African ensuring that the Negro does not visualise himself as an African but as an Antillean Negro/black. The race is then divided in its quest for whiteness thereby serving white hegemony. Fanon continues: "And yet many Antilles Negroes see nothing to upset them in such European identification; on the contrary, they find it altogether normal. That would be all we need, to be taken for niggers! The Europeans despise the Senegalese, and the Antilles Negro rules the black roost as its unchallenged master." (Fanon 1977 pg. 26). The Negro driven to escape being designated as nigger grabs hold of whiteness with the lust of the colonised and in so doing alienates himself from his race, from his being and divides his race and his being to ensure the sustainability of white hegemony. Fanon again states his research agenda for this chapter of the book which is instructive as follows: "We are trying to understand why the Antilles Negro is so fond of speaking French." (Fanon 1977 pg. 27). Fanon insists that this reality stems from being colonised which implants the futile quest to escape inferiority via embracing whiteness where you can never be white. You then reject your dialect/Creole for it's not a fit and proper language of the civilised and speaking it illustrates that you are not regenerated on the path to civilisation therefore in the state of being nigger. Our inferiority complex then negates the use and evolution of dialect/Creole as our language invented by us to express our worldview, transmit all that we are as a people and shore up our being with certainty. Fanon states: "It would seem, then, that the problem is this: In the Antilles, as in Brittany, there is a dialect and there is the French language. But this is false, for the Bretons do not consider themselves inferior to the French people. The Bretons have not been civilised by the white man." (Fanon 1977 pg. 28). The crux of the issue of the driving predisposition to become adept at the French language is located in the operational mechanism of white supremacist colonial discourse and its hegemony. Fanon persists in his position that the explanation lies in the inferiority complex of colonised peoples as follows: "What is there to say? Purely and simply this: When a bachelor of philosophy from the Antilles refuses to apply for certification as a teacher on the ground of his colour, I say that philosophy has never saved anyone. When someone else strives and strains to prove to me that black men are as intelligent as white men, I say that intelligence has never saved anyone; and that is true, for, if philosophy and intelligence are invoked to proclaim the equality of men, they have been employed to justify the extermination of men." (Fanon 1977 pgs. 28-29). Adept at the white man's knowledge and proclaimed to be as intelligent as the white man does and cannot dismantle the edifice/hierarchy of race based privilege and the impact on the quality of life of the non-white where life is granted even permitted for there is no right to non-white life hence Black Lives Matter. Being adept at the white man's knowledge, language and exhibiting his intelligence are all masks formulated to enable the operational effectiveness of white racism in its quest to exert hegemony over the non-whites of the world. A condition Fanon describes as follows: "I am speaking here, on the one hand, of alienated (duped) blacks, and, on the other, of no less alienated (duping and duped) whites." (Fanon 1977 pg. 29). Blacks and whites are both alienated and duped but only whites are doing the duping indicating the power relation of white hegemony. Fanon then retorts that his response will be of a nature external of black space and behaviour as follows: "And if I cry out, it will not be a black cry. No, from the point of view adopted here there is no black problem. Or at any rate if there is one it concerns the whites only accidentally." (Fanon 1977 pg. 29). Fanon does not locate himself in black space hence cannot emit a black cry neither can there be a black problem for white power creates the black problematic as its instrument of power against blacks. There is then only the white problematic and the threat it poses to non-white races of the world. Fanon's mission is then to solely address this reality: "What I want to do is help the black man to free himself of the arsenal of complexes that has been developed by the colonial environment." (Fanon 1977 pg. 30). To do this Fanon has first to liberate himself from the arsenal of complexes of white colonial domination and he expresses his liberation by insisting on his freedom operationally and perceptually from black-white space, epistemology, ontology and worldview. From Fanon there is no black cry and a black problem only an agenda for the liberation of a race.

Negro, Black, Nigger: Victim of an *Appearance*

Fanon now deals with the nature of what constitutes a Negro in the black-white complex. Fanon states: "To speak pidgin to a negro makes him angry because he himself is a pidgin-nigger-talker. But, I will be told, there is no wish, no intention to anger him. I grant this; but it is this absence of wish, this lack of interest, this indifference, this automatic manner of classifying him, imprisoning him, primitivising him, decivilising him, that makes him angry." (Fanon 1977 pg. 32). The white man speaks pidgin to the Negro simply because it is the language of the nigger. This position arises from a classificatory system that insists that the Negro is primitive and uncivilised which imprisons him in anger. This classificatory system is above the wilful intent of the whites who address the Negro with their version of pidgin as the utilisation of the instrument of the classificatory system is normal as it is a normalising instrument of white racist hegemonic discourse. A white racist normalising instrument insists that white racism is normal regardless of intent of the user. Fanon continues: "When it comes to the case of the Negro, nothing of the kind. He has no culture, no civilisation, no 'long historical past.'" "Willy-nilly the Negro has to wear the livery that the white man has sewed for him." (Fanon 1977 pg. 34). "Yes, the black man is supposed to be a good nigger; once this has been laid down, the rest follows of itself. To make him talk pidgin is to fasten him to the effigy of him, to snare him, to imprison him, the eternal victim of an essence, of an *appearance* for which he is not responsible." Fanon 1977 pg. 35). The white man constitutes the nigger by creating an essence, an *appearance* that envelops the body and persona of the Negro/the black man for the comfort and security of the white man. The white man then expects all negroes to abide by the normalising demands of this soul by being fully compliant and responsive niggers. For the white man the only interest is compliance for the soul of the nigger fastened to the Negro/the black man is policed by the white power structure. For the Negro/the black man the central issue is always the constant dynamic stress between the drive to liberation and the drive to compliance wherein the need to live on a daily basis results in shades of grey between both extremes. Fanon continues: "What I am asserting is that the European has a fixed concept of the Negro, and there is nothing more exasperating than to be asked: 'How long have you been in France? You speak French so well?'" (Fanon 1977 pg. 35). For Fanon this is illustrated by whites speaking their version of pidgin nigger to the Negro in apparent disregard to the French spoken to them by the Negro. Fanon states: "No, speaking pidgin-nigger closes off the black man; it perpetuates a state of conflict in which the white man injects the black with extremely dangerous foreign bodies. Nothing is more astonishing than to hear a black man express himself properly, for there in truth he is putting on the white world." (Fanon 1977 pg. 36). The black man in Europe conversant and versed in white language and culture poses a dilemma to the white power structure hence a threat. White racist hegemony demands power relations where they exert hegemony over all non-white races and one path to this is the assault of the black/non-white-white relation on non-white races. This strategy calls for the formulation and attachment of white souls on black/non-white bodies and perceptions towards constituting dual personalities housed in a body. But on the ground in North Atlantic white dominated societies the sought ideal product of the white-black relation poses a threat to whites, as the negro is not supposed to be able to absorb and exhibit instances of white culture and language as they are inherently inferior. This is the product of the operationalisation of the discourse of white racist supremacy, which is posing in the 21st century a grave threat to the effectiveness of the mechanism of white racist power manifested through the black-white relation. In this event the white power structure resorts to policing the non-whites of the North Atlantic via fascist and National Socialist discourses as is clearly illustrated in the North Atlantic of the 21st century. Fanon states: "It is understandable that the first action of the black man is a *reaction*, and, since the Negro is appraised in terms of his assimilation, it is also understandable why the newcomer only expresses himself in French. It is because he wants to emphasise the rupture that has now occurred." (Fanon 1977 pg. 36). The Negro faced with white racism in Europe reacts by indicating his command of white culture and language with the expectation that his whiteness will purchase acceptance from white folks. When his whiteness fails to purchase space and the embrace of the whites in the white mainstream the Negro realises that all he can embrace are the banlieues or non-white spaces allocated to them by the white power structure. The black man, all non-whites living in the white dominated societies of the North Atlantic who choose whiteness as a strategy are duped, were duped and will continue to be duped for the white power structure is much more than the black-white relation for the whites are also duped whilst they are doing the duping. The choice for the non-whites in Europe for Fanon is as follows: "they have the choice of two possibilities: -either to stand with the white world...or to reject Europe, 'Yo', and cling together in their dialect, making themselves quite comfortable in what we shall call the *Umwelt* of Martinique." (Fanon 1977 pg. 37). The white power structure by the presence of the non-white in white dominated terrain is pursuing the strategy of alienating space to designate as non-white spaces which will visibly attest to the hierarchical superiority of the white over non-whites in all its deprivation. Will blacks of Martinique then create their Umwelt within the confines of these banlieues confirming the inherent inferiority of blacks and justifying their detention in internal colonies? This then is a twisted and distorted Umwelt indicative of the colonial domination of Martinique replicated in France. It must always be recognised that the banlieues of Europe are not primarily constructed as holding bays for infectious non-white races but as a potent indicator to white folks that the white power structure is protecting their culture, language, heritage and way of life from the assault of and infection by inferior races. This order of internal colonialism then demands white compliance and servility to the dictates of the white power structure. This is simply social control utilising racism and a typology of races. The black-white relation/complex is then an instrument of power, formulated and driven by a strategy of power which necessitates the exposure and operationalisation of the power relations and the psychoexistential complex. Fanon ends this chapter of the book by recapping his premise stated at the outset as follows: "As I said at the start, there is a retaining-wall relation between language and group. To speak a language is to take on a world, a culture. The Antilles Negro who wants to be white will be the whiter as he gains greater mastery of the cultural tool that language is." (Fanon 1977 pg. 38). Is liberation then possible? Liberation from what?

To leave the colony of the West Indies, where whites are a visible powered minority facing a non-white majority, where the hegemony of the metropole and the white oligarchy of the colony is assured by the compliance of the non-white majority; and enter the social order of the metropole, where the non-white is now the visible powerless minority, triggers the quest for and the belief that the white metropole affords space, opportunity and necessity for immersion of the non-white in whiteness. The black soul is embraced and worn with gusto and pride driven by the expectation of rewards for being a regenerated and assimilated black man. When the expectations prove hollow and unfulfilled the response falls within a spectrum of fatalism driven by self-hate and racism towards non-whites and whites. This then is the vast black abyss. Fanon in his search for the point of liberation that is demanded in his findings of this book would in his following two books insist that liberation is not to be found via migration to the metropole nor via the black-white complex in the colonies, but only via revolution in the colonies and the former colonies. Fanon will insist that only revolution waged against the coloniser can and will cleanse the colonised of our debilitating black soul for only violence is the cleansing force necessary to destroying the black soul and liberating the pre-colonisation person trapped within. Violence is necessary as colonisation is a most violent process. Fanon provides the answer to the question raised in this book in the book that followed: "A Dying Colonialism" which defined his project after "Black skin, White Masks." The analysis of a psychoexistential complex must now be buttressed by a revolutionary praxis driven by a revolutionary discourse which completed Fanon's project and his quest. Within this revolutionary praxis and discourse there was no primacy afforded to the issue of non-whites in the white metropole. As Fanon made his pilgrimage from the white metropole, France, to the Algerian revolution, and made his contribution to the revolution and its success, others as Fanon can emulate!

Chapter 3
Whiteness, the Black Woman and the White Man

Authentic Love and the Inferiority Complex

This chapter analyses chapter two of Fanon's book under study in which Fanon utilises the deconstruction of the content of books of relevance to the topic. Fanon expresses his agenda in this chapter as follows: "In this chapter devoted to the relations between the woman of colour and the European, it is our problem to ascertain to what extent authentic love will remain unattainable before one has purged oneself of that feeling of inferiority or that Adlerian exaltation, that overcompensation, which seems to be the indices of the black Weltanschaaung." (Fanon 1977 pg. 42). Fanon is insisting that the inferiority complex of non-whites is the classificatory measure of the worldview of non-whites. The inferiority complex illustrates and orders all that forming the non-white worldview which is constituted by white supremacist hegemonic discourse. Fanon is then exploring the mechanism of a black woman burdened with an inferiority complex generated by the black-white complex finding authentic love in a relationship with a white male. Raising the question of the attainability of authentic love whilst the black woman is burdened with the black-white complex. To do this Fanon first deconstructs the book "Je suis Martiniquaise" by Mayotte Capecia stating: "Mayotte loves a white man to whom she submits in everything. He is her lord. She asks nothing, demands nothing, except a bit of whiteness in her life." (Fanon 1977 pg. 42). Fanon in deconstructing Mayotte's reasons given in her book for loving the white man says that her hierarchy of reasons was as follows: blue eyes, blond hair and a light skin. The man was everything Mayotte was not physically and longed to be. Mayotte then settled for a vicarious expression of being white, my man is white I am now white, and the joy of possessing by proximity and privacy a white man and his whiteness. The blackest thing on my white man is his kaka (asshole) hole. For this Mayotte surrendered to the white man she then adopted the power relation of a slave being intimate with massa on his plantation. She lost herself in the white man as her black self was worthless and the best possible outcome was to lose it in a white man's persona.

The Quest for Whiteness

Fanon through Mayotte Capecia's book presents the link between inferiority and class position in the case of Martinique as follows: "It was Didier, the preserve of the richest people in Martinique, that magnetised all the girl's wishes. And she makes the point herself: One is white above a certain financial level. The houses in this section have long dazzled the lady." (Fanon 1977 pg. 44). Didier as the spatial expression of white power summed up Mayotte's conviction that it was only via being attached to a white man can she attain a presence in Didier. Fanon is describing the impact of the conjunction of race and class (race/class) in the West Indies on the worldview of the blacks in the West Indies. Fanon continues on this reality: "It is in fact customary in Martinique to dream of a form of salvation that consists of magically turning white. A house in Didier, acceptance into that high society" (Fanon 1977 pg. 44). To turn white is a multi-purpose strategy as you escape your class position and become whitened thereby resulting in the position that whiteness and whitening is the best possible path to liberation from a class position driven by deprivation. Mayotte's entry into Didier is premised entirely on being the black appendage of her white man and her expectation of acceptance is destroyed for a black appendage is simply not white and can never be white. Fanon states: "Her resentment feeds on her own artificiality. We shall see why love is beyond the reach of the Mayotte Capecias of all nations. For the beloved should not allow me to turn my infantile fantasies into reality. On the contrary, he should help me to go beyond them." (Fanon 1977 pg. 44). Mayotte is executing a strategy to break out of the space allocated to her in the social order because of her skin with its accompanying class position, but there is no certainty that her white man, that she has surrendered totally to, is in possession of authentic love for her. Her white man can in fact be viewing Mayotte as his trophy who renders service to him in a manner and of a desired quality that no white woman is willing to. Whilst in white company white men ask him about the quality of sexual relations with his black trophy as Mayotte's white man projects his "liberalism," distinction and difference to all and sundry for when you go black you never go back. It is then a dual dynamic which raises the question of: What's love got to do with it? Fanon continues his analysis of Mayotte: "It would seem indeed that her white and black represent the two poles of a world, two poles in perpetual conflict: a genuinely Manichean concept of the world; the word has been spoken, it must be remembered-white or black that is the question." (Fanon 1977 pgs. 44-45). Again: "So, since she could no longer try to blacken, to negrify the world she was going to try, in her own body and in her own mind, to bleach it." (Fanon 1977 pg. 45). Mayotte's Manichean worldview demands that she first attempt to turn her world black but this failed miserably given the power relations of the race/class structure of Martinique. She then moved to whiten her mind and her body, but sadly her body despite all attempts to chemically and physically alter it, will and can never be white and this tears at her so she settles for her white mind, her white man and most important of all the quest for Miscegenated children. Fanon describes the narcissism of the Manichean condition as follows: "And there one lies body to body with one's blackness or one's whiteness, in full narcissistic cry, each sealed into his own peculiarity-with, it is true, now and then a flash or so, but these are threatened at their source." (Fanon 1977 pg. 45). In Mayotte's case the quest to whiten is in fact a quest for survival and its strategy driven by her narcissism. In this quest Mayotte must then genetically dilute her blackness which establishes her fitness for whiteness so she discovers her white grandmother who dared cross the racial divide by copulating and procreating with a black man. Mayotte has then the genetic lineage to seek out only a white man as her mother is a mulatto woman and she is seeking to wash the African from her genetic code some two generations in the future. Mayotte is then a Caribbean eugenicist actively pursuing the praxis of Caribbean eugenics produced by the power relations of the plantation. Fanon states: "Instead of recognising her absolute blackness, she proceeds to turn it into an accident. She learns that her grandmother was white." (Fanon 1977 pg. 46). "We are put on notice that what Mayotte wants is a kind of lactification. For, in a word, the race must be whitened; every woman in Martinique knows this, says it, repeats it." (Fanon 1977 pg. 47). Mayotte's strategy is then common and affirmed as it is common to the social order in the spaces dominated by the majority black race of Martinique. Fanon insists that it in fact seeks to normalise female behaviour as follows: "The number of sayings, proverbs, petty rules of conduct that govern the choice of a lover in the Antilles is astounding. It is always essential to avoid falling back into the pit of niggerhood, and every woman in the Antilles, whether in a casual flirtation or in a serious affair, is determined to select the least black of the men." (Fanon 1977 pg. 47). In response to white supremacist discourse and its mechanism of power operationalised through its instruments of power expressed as the black-white complex, Antillean blacks have created a hierarchy of blackness premised on a gradation of skin colour visualised. This hierarchy of blackness then determines the desirability and attractiveness of an individual black man or woman. The apex of the pyramid will then be those of the Miscegenated in a descending order to those with the blackest skin colour which enforces the quest for whiteness and copulation across the racist divide. The order of the colour hierarchy based on measured fractions of a white bloodline established by the white massa to define and classify in a hierarchical order the enslaved of the plantation lives on in the Antilles of Fanon. This hierarchy of blackness utilised by the blacks of Martinique to police and normalise human behaviour entails the exercise of black on black racism driven by self-hate and the need to create the other's other. This divides a besieged black race in a racist social order against itself deflecting its gaze away from the nature of power relations by insisting that the enemy is your fellow blacks whilst the only route to emancipation is with the massa. This then is the terrain where black on black eugenics is practised as the solution especially illustrated in multi-racial countries of the Caribbean where black on black racism frames the other's other as another black race stimulating the evolution of a potent strain of black eugenics and the politics of racist hegemony. Mayotte exemplifies this black eugenics praxis by first acquiring her white man and then producing a half breed child, a miscegenated child vital to her task of purging her bloodline of its African genetic code thereby washing it to whiteness as the laundry she laundered at one time. Mayotte is well on her way to erase the mistakes her white maternal grand-mother and her mother made summed up in the physical and iconographic existence and survival of Mayotte's half white child. This child sends the potent message to black women who have no half breed child of Mayotte's inherent superiority, of her whiteness and in the company of black women Mayotte will send potent messages of her inherent difference and that of her child. In public Mayotte will play with her child's hair illustrating that this hair is not Negro hair not "hard" hair but "soft" hair, she will insist that her half breed child not play with niggers as they will bully, brutalise and infect her/him with nigger ways and she will insist that she/he doesn't play in the sun as she/he will get black/dark. The half breed child then is a trophy, a talisman, and the potential of a path where successive generations of Mayotte's offspring can be white as driven snow. Mayotte simply is not fazed by the reality that her white man impregnates her and moves on as he leaves in her care his greatest gift: the miscegenated child. Mayotte will rail at the tendency of black men to impregnate black women and abandon their black children and black women but such judgement simply does not apply to Mayotte's white man for his is the right to conquer and move on to another conquest.

Phobic Behaviour and Affect

Fanon now deals specifically with the psychology of the blacks of this milieu as follows: "We must see whether it is possible for the black man to overcome his feeling of insignificance, to rid his life of the compulsive quality that makes it so like behaviour of the phobic. Affect is exacerbated in the Negro, he is full of rage because he feels small, he suffers from an inadequacy in all human communication, and all these factors chain him with an unbearable insularity." (Fanon 1977 pg. 50). The phobic behaviour Fanon alludes to is the compulsive actions that arise from the conviction of insignificance and the rage that flows from said compulsive behaviour. The inferiority complex enhanced and intensified by the hierarchy of blackness with its spectrum of grades of blackness enhances the affect where the gaze of the blacks in this hierarchy are turned inwards on each other giving rise to a singularity limited in expanse which drives the insularity of its inmates. The inferiority complex impacts the choice of specific types of behaviour in an attempt at forging a survival strategy that enhances the affect of the black-white relation, primarily because the means used to forge the survival strategy is the product of white hegemonic power and its mechanism of power which constitutes the black as the white man's Other. Fanon continues: "We understand now why the black man cannot take pleasure in his insularity. For him there is only one way out, and it leads into the white world. Whence his constant preoccupation with attracting the attention of the white man, his concern with being powerful like the white man...As I said earlier, it is from within that the Negro will seek admittance to the white sanctuary. This attitude derives from the intention." (Fanon 1977 pg. 51). There is no insularity predicated on being a self-loving and self-affirming human for black insularity is a defence mechanism and in the face of the quest to be white and to be affirmed by the white man it is a strategy of offence where you alienate yourself from the competition for entry into whiteness and white affirmation. You alienate yourself from your race and your being in the quest for whiteness and white affirmation. At the level of desire, the black human surrenders to the white affect having had the intention to surrender installed as part of the perceptual furniture of the constituted black human. But at the point of surrender our actions are futile and we live lives of grave futility as we can never be white!

Hate, Discrimination and Negrophobia

Fanon then presents his analysis of hate, specifically hatred for the black human by whites as follows: "I have said that Negrophobes exist. It is not hatred of the Negro, however, that motivates them; they lack the courage for that, or they have lost it. Hate is not inborn; it has to be constantly cultivated, to be brought into being, in conflict with more or less recognised guilt complexes. Hate demands existence, and he who hates has to show his hate in appropriate actions and behaviour; in a sense he has to become hate. That is why the Americans have substituted discrimination for lynching. Each to his own side of the street." (Fanon 1977 pg. 53). Fanon insists that there exists Negrophobes and Negrophobia but the basis of this specific entity is not hatred for the black human for they are separate and apart. Hatred for the black human has to be created and cultivated as it is not a human genetic trait and it demands to be expressed via actions and behaviour that express effectively its nature. The human who hates has then to be consumed by hate and must evolve into an active agent expressing this hate. Hate then demands violent action against the human framed as the recipient of hate, which necessitates that the vehicle of hate overcome the existing structure of guilt complexes that impact the intention of the human vehicle of hate in action. In light of these specific realities of hate and its impact on the social order the first choice of the strategy is discrimination as in the USA and other North Atlantic societies where discrimination, Negrophobia and hate exist and impact the social order simultaneously and conjointly whilst exercising a power dynamic amongst themselves in a quest for hegemony. The nature of this dynamic is then of utmost importance towards understanding race, racism and the social order of the North Atlantic. What is apparent in the 21st century is the appearance of the bid by hate for hegemony driven by the paranoia of white folks over a clear and present danger to their culture, life style and hegemony posed by the non-whites with: the demographic threat posed in the USA with the imminent eclipse of whites as the majority race of the USA by non-whites, the threat of Islam and Islamic extremism to North Atlantic white hegemony and security and non-white, Muslim migration to Europe. White paranoid fear is then driving the bid by hate for hegemony over discrimination and Negro/non-white phobia. This drive for hegemony by hate is expressed via discourses of white supremacy and its political discourses of Fascism and National Socialism.

Affective Erethism

Fanon then returns to his methodology of deconstructing a work with his choice being "Nini" by Abdoulaye Sadji. Fanon states: "Analysing various passages of Abdoulaye Sadji's story; I shall attempt to grasp the living reactions of the woman of colour to the European. First of all, there are two such women: The Negress and the mulatto. The first has only one possibility and one concern: to turn white. The second wants not only to turn white but also to avoid slipping back. What indeed could be more illogical than a mulatto woman's acceptance of a Negro husband? For it must be understood once and for all that it is a question of saving the race." (Fanon 1977 pgs.54-55). Fanon differentiates between the agenda of the Negress and that of the mulatto as the miscegenated is not only seeking whiteness but also to evade washing the white genetic code out of her bloodline. Fanon illustrates this by deconstructing Sadji's story of Nini the mulatto stenographer who is being courted by Maktar a black man. Fanon states: "Maktar makes himself the slave of Nini, the mulatto. The mulatto considers his letter an insult, an outrage to her honour as a 'white lady.' This Negro is an idiot, a scoundrel, an ignoramus who needs a lesson. That lesson she is prepared to give him; she will teach him to be more courteous and less brazen; she will make him understand that 'white skins' are not for 'bougnouls'. Having learned the circumstances, the whole mulatto 'society' plays chorus for her wrath." (Fanon 1977 pg. 56). Nini is delusional by mistaking her allotted place in the black on black hierarchy she imagines that it applies to the white-black hierarchy. In the black on black hierarchy she can demand that she is white, but in the white-black hegemonic hierarchy she presents the most potent threat to and the gravest dilemma presented to the white-black hierarchy by procreation across the racist divide. Nini can demand her "whiteness" only to black people not to white people placing her in a precarious state of human existence. This is then a mulatto strategy in an attempt to wield power over the blacks of the racist social order and to demand from the hegemonic whites their rightful place in the white-black hierarchy befitting those with a white parent. Mulattoes must then be in perpetual denial of either of or both their genetic origins. Fanon then presents the case of Dedee who was the recipient of a marriage proposal from the white man M. Darrivey. Fanon states: "Something remarkable must have happened on the day when the white man declared his love to the mulatto. There was recognition, incorporation into a group that had seemed hermetic. The psychological minus-value, this feeling of insignificance and its corollary, the impossibility of reaching the light, totally vanished. From one day to the next, the mulatto went from the class of slaves to that of masters. She had been recognised through her overcompensating behaviour. She was no longer the woman who wanted to be white; she was white. She was joining the white world." (Fanon 1977 pg. 58). Dedee with the marriage proposal from the white man has been now given the opportunity to cast her black genetic code aside as she has finally breached the white barrier that denies access to the halcyon fields of whiteness which part of her genetic code entitled her to. This was all in Dedee's mind as the product of a hope and longing which hatched delusion, for it was not premised on the reality of power relations within the white-black hierarchy governing the miscegenated. Dedee is then gravely duped to an extent that surpasses and eclipses that of Mayotte. Fanon states on Dedee as follows: "But in Dedee's case the ego does not have to defend itself, since its claims have been officially recognised: She is marrying a white man." (Fanon 1977 pg. 59). Dedee has no need to defend her ego as her dreams for definition and anchoring of self in whiteness have now materialised and have been realised as reality thanks to the action, not of Dedee but of a white man. Forever insular, insignificant, small and passive in the hope for whiteness, which remains just a hope for only white action can afford this hope some form of reality and realisation. Fanon then insists that in the case of Mayotte, Nini and Dedee the process is the same. Fanon states: "A bilateral process, an attempt to acquire-by internalising them-assets that were originally prohibited. It is because the Negress feels inferior that she aspires to win admittance into the white world. In this endeavour she will seek the help of a phenomenon that we shall call *affective erethism.*" (Fanon 1977 pg. 60). The entry of the mulatto woman and the Negress into the white world is not a unilateral process for they simply do not satisfy the entry requirements. The mulatto woman and the Negress must then attract and convince a white man that she is worth the cost that will be levied on him of doing so. Fanon insists that in this quest for whiteness both the mulatto woman and the Negress must resort to the tools afforded by affective erethism. Affective erethism deconstructed yields: affective: refers to moods, feelings and attitudes. Refers to mental disorders where the primary symptom is the disturbance of moods. Erethism: a neurological disorder characterised by excessive sensitivity or rapid reaction to stimulation and a state of abnormal mental excitement or irritation. Placed in the context of the text Fanon is then indicating that in the pursuit of whiteness the black woman can only strategically pursue said liberation in a mental and emotional condition that is flawed, even plagued with disorders. For the liberation fixated on is not substantially liberating as whiteness is achieved only in the mind of the black woman, but in actual power relations she willingly accepts servility and other relational conditions that she blatantly refuses to accept from a black male. In addition, the black woman pursues the dream of liberation via a white male as a fixation with no reference to the actual reality of attaining such an end. Bundled together this impacts the mental health of the black woman where she exhibits the symptoms of affective erethism or a specific form of colonised bipolarity.

Neurotic Orientation

Fanon as the chapter closes sums up his analysis as follows: "The Negro enslaved by his inferiority, the white man by his superiority alike behave in accordance with a neurotic orientation. The Negro's behaviour makes him akin to an obsessive neurotic type, or, if one prefers, he puts himself into a complete situational neurosis. In the man of colour there is a constant effort to run away from his own individuality, to annihilate his own presence. Whenever a man of colour protests, there is alienation. Whenever a man of colour rebukes there is alienation. We shall see later, that the Negro, having been made inferior, proceeds from humiliating insecurity through strongly voiced self-accusation to despair. The attitude of the black man toward the white or his own race, often duplicates almost completely a constellation of delirium, frequently bordering on the region of the pathological." (Fanon 1977 pg. 60). The white-black complex manifests itself in a neurotic orientation where the Negro is trapped in an operational neurosis where the Negro flees individuality seeking to erase all traces of her/his presence where despair is the reward for such actions. For the Negro is incapable of assertive action free of the limitation and encumbrance of alienation for she/he remains trapped in a structure of delirium that frames, conditions and limits all action. Fanon insists that all of these issues flow from the Negro being made inferior but what is noteworthy with Fanon's analysis is the state and condition of powerlessness he describes. Powerlessness that flows from a psychological structure that renders independent human action problematic at best and from a relational condition of power relations where they are constituted as suppliant to the dominance of the whites. The psychological structure and the power relations are expressed in then a race/class structure where the suppliant blacks dominate the poorest and most deprived population of the social order and the whites dominate the oligarchy in the Caribbean island chain, where blacks dominate the demography of the islands in the 21st century. In the English speaking Caribbean island chain in specific islands since independence, other minority races as Chinese and Arabs have joined the ranks of the oligarchy whilst the Africans remain excluded, such as in Jamaica. A fundamental issue is the demography of the islands which determines the supply of whites available for relationships with blacks. Of much greater impact is the deliberate policing of members of race minority groups who dominate the oligarchy to ensure that the wealth accumulation drive of the family and clan remains within the family across generations and the family retains the genetic identity of its founding couples. Race and family kinship ties are managed across generations via selective breeding which embraces marrying your cousins. Males of these minority oligarchic race groups face severe reprimand, even exclusion, for marrying out of the desired pool and for a female it means being excommunicated, cut off from the wealth and power the family wields. Black women desirous and in pursuit of a relationship with members of these oligarchic families are faced then with a grave shortage of available males provided they are willing to settle for much less than what Mayotte received from her white man. The oligarchic families of the Caribbean island chain have then formulated and operationalised a strategy to counter and render mute the threat posed by miscegenation. You literally lose everything you have grown accustomed to, especially the power and impunity of your family you have grown to love and expect. The alternative is then to seek out the foreign white man following the Mayotte strategy, but work for the exodus from the Caribbean with the foreign white man. Or simply enjoy it while it lasts as there is always a pressing expectation of end, finality of a dream never fully realised.

Fanon in this chapter sketches a multifaceted approach necessary to understand Caribbean reality. He is focusing on psychoanalysis and psychiatric analysis whilst being mindful of the social structure, but the analytical approach will only be complete with an understanding of the power relations that hold this social order together which gives space to the actions of the individual in a social context. The focus is on individuals in a social context which demands analysis of the social context in terms of power/force relations and hegemony.

Chapter 4
Sexual Preoccupation, the Black Man and the White Woman

The Zebra Striping of My Mind

Fanon commences chapter three of his work by stating as follows: "Out of the darkest part of my soul, across the zebra striping of my mind, surges this desire to be suddenly *white*. I wish to be acknowledged not as *black* but as *white*. Now...who but a white woman can do this for me? By loving me she proves that I am worthy of white love. I am loved like a white man. I am a white man. Her love takes me onto the noble road that leads to total realisation. I marry white culture, white beauty, white whiteness. When my restless hands caress those white breasts, they grasp white civilisation and dignity and make them mine." (Fanon 1977 pg. 63). The mind is zebra striped, neither fully black nor white, hence the quest for whiteness is unfulfilled and cannot be self-sustained nor accomplished from the resource base of the zebra striped mind. An input of whiteness is then crucial from an external source and ideally from a white woman who showers the zebra striped mind with whiteness. This then is the act of love sought and which only a white partner can bestow for the quest is not only to be white, but to possess white civilisation and to do so I must possess the white woman for she is my trophy illustrating I am civilised. But in spite of the white trophy and the ability to manipulate what you consider to be symbols, instruments even metrics of white civilisation and high bred whiteness we remain non-white, black. It simply does not matter how effectively we have mastered the task of being white our skins, our genetic code remains non-white, black. The skin is presented for scrutiny and reaction long before the whiteness beneath the skin and it is the skin that triggers the automatic grasp for the stereotypes, the Negrophobia, to define and sum up the black man in terms comprehensible and comfortable to white people rendering all the whiteness beneath the skin moot at best. Hence the fixation with altering the skin, with constantly masking the skin by being disciples of the cult of white fashion and the fetish of the presentation of the presentable, acceptable body to the all penetrating gaze.

The Lamb to be Slaughtered

Fanon in this chapter continues with the methodology of deconstructing written works and he commences with "Un homme pareil aux autres" by Rene Maran by focusing on the character Jean Veneuse of the work. Fanon states: "What are the terms of the problem? Jean Veneuse is a Negro. Born in the Antilles, he has lived in Bordeaux for years; so he is a European. But he is black; so he is a Negro. There is the conflict. He does not understand his own race, and the whites do not understand him." (Fanon 1977 pg. 64). Fanon continues "Unable to be assimilated, unable to pass unnoticed, he consoles himself by associating with the dead, or at least the absent." (Fanon 1977 pg. 65). Veneuse views the world through the cultural and perceptive apparatus of the white man but he cannot blend into the white mass, in a crowd, in the daily transactional basis of his life he simply cannot be another human in the mass flow of human transactions for he is black, a Negro. Veneuse is alienated from the white mass he shares a worldview with, he is alienated from his race as they don't share his white worldview or better put, they are not as white as him. In his quest for white anonymity Veneuse delves deeply into and finds solitude in white history and culture perfecting his cultured white worldview thereby intensifying his alienation. Fanon continues: "Above all, he wants to prove to the others that he is a man, their equal. But let us not be misled: Jean Veneuse is the man who has to be convinced. It is the roots of his soul, as complicated as that of any European, that the doubt persists. If the expression may be allowed, Jean Veneuse is the lamb to be slaughtered. Let us make the effort." (Fanon 1977 pg. 66). Veneuse wants to be accepted as a man but he remains to be convinced that he is a man because of his total immersion in a worldview and its cultural apparatus that denies his manhood. This whiteness denies his humanity placing the antinomy at the roots of his soul, placed there by the sophism of whiteness internalised by a non-white. Veneuse's dedication to the embrace of white culture eventually leads to a white woman indicating to him in writing that she loved him and Veneuse insists that he must have the permission of her brother to marry her. Fanon states:

"When the question is put directly, then, the white man agrees to give his sister to the black-but on one condition: You have nothing in common with real Negroes. You are not black but 'extremely brown.' 'You're 'us,'' Coulanges tells him; and if anyone thinks you are a Negro he is mistaken, because you merely look like one. But Jean Veneuse does not want this. He cannot accept it, because he knows. He knows that, 'enraged by this degrading ostracism, mulattoes and Negroes have only one thought from the moment they land in Europe: to gratify their appetite for white women.'" (Fanon 1977 pg. 69). The white man expresses the ambivalence of the condition of existence of a black viewing the world through a white worldview. Your skin defines you regardless of your whiteness and all your efforts at embracing whiteness leaves you at the mercy of the white man to recognize your hard work at becoming white by placing you in a category of being better than a "real Negro" but less than, never white for Veneuse is simply "extremely brown." Whiteness has diluted the blackness of the Negro to the point where Veneuse is "extremely brown" but can never be white as the nigger core remains and persists in spite of the best efforts of Veneuse to purge, wash it away with whiteness. As long as the non-white seeks the affirmation of whiteness, the approbation of the white man, there will be no active, human individual in pursuit of her/his goals rooted in a hegemonic concept of self-confidence and self-love rooted in a worldview where the individual is at the centre of the universe. Veneuse shares his worldview with a white man who exercises hegemony over Veneuse, which denies Veneuse self-confidence and self-love for Veneuse is a tenant in his own worldview and a slave in its operational reality. For Veneuse in his whiteness renders himself ever in search of white approbation and definition which denies him human self-determination. The only choice the racist structure offers Veneuse is to copulate with a white woman, but this in itself is subject to the policing of the white man with a history of graphic violence. Veneuse recognises the pitfalls of the pursuit of white women maybe because to do this will illustrate his un-regenerated nigger core and the power of influence it exercises over him in spite of his great effort to embrace whiteness. Faced with this conundrum Veneuse chooses to enter into the colonial service in Africa.

Fanon analyses Veneuse's rationale for entering the African colonial service as follows: "What a struggle to free himself of a purely subjective conflict. I am a white man, I was born in Europe, all my friends are white. There are not eight Negroes in the city where I live. I think in French, France is my religion. I am a European do you understand? I am not a Negro, and in order to prove it to you, I as a public employee am going to show the genuine Negroes the differences that separate me from them." (Fanon 1977 pg. 70). Veneuse is not an extremely brown negro he is not a negro period for he is white, French and a French patriot but also born in Europe and a European. To illustrate his whiteness Veneuse will enter the French colonial service of Africa and exercise French racist colonial domination, in its operational diversity over the original real Negroes, the source of all niggers. Veneuse is then another model or type of the compradors of the West Indian slave plantations who all willingly, above and beyond the call of enslavement, served massa's quest for sustainable hegemony over the enslaved. A long line of compradors that flourishes to this day, that continue to serve massa in spite of unrequited love. Veneuse served as a colonial massa in Africa with distinction and then left to return to his beloved France potently illustrating to the Africans that he was not an African, not a Negro, not a nigger, but a colonial official exercising white colonial racist power with relish, whilst encumbered with a black skin. What then was Veneuse is the mystery to solve.

The Cinderella Complex

Fanon floats the concept of sexual preoccupation in reference to the black man's fixation with sexual intercourse with a white woman then he moves on (Fanon 1977 pg. 72). Fanon states that Veneuse exhibits the following: "The attitude is one recrimination toward the past, devaluation of self, incapability of being understood as he would like to be." (Fanon 1977 pg. 74). Fanon insists that Veneuse has an abandonment-neurotic. Fanon states that Veneuse has a Cinderella complex. (Fanon pg. 77). Fanon sums up his analysis of Veneuse as follows: "Jean Veneuse is a neurotic, and his colour is only an attempt to explain his psychic structure. If this objective difference had not existed, he would have manufactured it out of nothing. Jean Veneuse is one of those intellectuals who try to take a position solely on the level of the ideas." "Well, it is clear to me that Jean Veneuse, alias Rene Maran, is neither more or less than a black abandonment-neurotic. And he is put back into his place, his proper place.

He is a neurotic who needs to be emancipated from his infantile fantasies. And I contend that Jean Veneuse represents not an example of black-white relations, but a certain mode of behaviour in a neurotic who by coincidence is black." (Fanon 1977 pg. 79). Veneuse is primarily a neurotic who uses his colour as the excuse for his neurotic behaviour. Veneuse is not constituted by the black-white relations/complex but by his childhood experiences, which he then rationalised as being the result of his blackness. But does this position exonerate the black-white complex from its impact on Veneuse and the manner he interpreted this impact through his neurotic operational worldview where the specificity of a black abandonment-neurotic is constituted? Fanon presents no answers as it is out of the scope of the work under analysis. But Fanon does state as follows: "The neurotic structure of an individual is simply the elaboration, the formation, the eruption within the ego, of conflictual cultures arising in part out of the environment and in part out of the purely personal way the individual reacts to these influences." (Fanon 1977 pg. 81). The white racism that has impacted Veneuse throughout his life has impacted his ego and Veneuse has interpreted these conflicts and manifested an operational response that is neurotic in part, in response to a white racist assault. Veneuse is then more than a neurotic who is black, but a black who has manifested neurotic behaviour as a strategic response to white racist assault on a black abandoned child. If Veneuse was white, then he would simply be neurotic for there would have been no white racist assault. Fanon then offers insight into his position by stating as follows: "Just as there was a touch of fraud in trying to deduce from the behaviour of Nini and Mayotte Capecia a general law of the behaviour of the black woman with the white man, there would be a similar lack of objectivity, I believe, in trying to extend the attitude of Veneuse to the man of colour as such." (Fanon 1977 pg. 81). Fanon's methodology utilised in the two chapters is not seeking to constitute general laws of behaviour of black women and men with white partners. Fanon's intent is to illustrate that in the cases cited the behaviour exhibited arose not from the black skin, but in reaction to white racist assault on the black persona. Fanon states: "And I should like to think that I have discouraged any endeavours to connect the defeats of Jean Veneuse with the greater or lesser concentration of melanin in his epidermis." (Fanon 1977 pg. 81). Jean Veneuse is neurotic not because of being black, but as the product of white racist assault on his black persona. Being black is not pathological, but being black in a world where white racist discourse, power/ knowledge is hegemonic is a combination with a predilection for emotional problems.

Sexual Myth and Separation

Fanon ends this chapter by stating as follows: "This sexual myth-the quest for white flesh-perpetuated by alienated psyches, must no longer be allowed to impede active understanding. In no way should my colour be regarded as a flaw. From the moment the Negro accepts the separation imposed by the European he has no further respite, and 'is it not understandable that thenceforward he will try to elevate himself to the white man's level? To elevate himself in the range of colours to which he attributes a kind of hierarchy?' We shall see that another solution is possible. It implies a restructuring of the world." (Fanon 1977 pgs. 81-82). The alienated psyches pursue white flesh and posture the black craving for white flesh which is an impediment to understanding, which confirms the sexual myths and racist stereotypes where a specific black sexuality is constituted and affixed to the black body which cannot enable understanding of the power dynamics involved. For Fanon insists that acceptance of the separation, the alienation, that surrender to the white man's black-white complex bestows places the black on a futile quest for equality and parity with the white man which is a futile quest unless we can change our genetic code. The relentless quest which is encapsulated in a hierarchy of colours, where the non-white can never find the exit, because the hierarchy is fluid and dynamic as it responds to the power relations between hegemonic whites and supplicant non-whites. This is then the white man's matrix where he persistently shifts the goalposts. Fanon gestures at the solution by insisting that rather than accepting the white man's racist separation of the races/apartheid we must restructure the world or invoke revolution to purge us of the propensity of the colonised to willingly embrace the separation. In this chapter and the previous one Fanon utilises white racist medical discourse with its psychological and psychoanalytical theorising to unearth the impact of white racism on the black psyche. This is a conundrum at best, at worst it is using white supremacist discourse as an instrument of liberation of non-whites. Fanon makes repeated references to Hegel in the work under analysis, the very same Hegel noted for his white racist discourse. Fanon emancipates himself from this trap by formulating and operationalising revolutionary psychoanalysis and psychiatry within a revolutionary context; the Algerian Revolution seen in his second work: "A Dying Colonialism" where he presents the position hinted at in "Black Skin, White Masks." That it is only within a revolutionary context that the colonised can be liberated from the burden of colonisation. It is then necessary to become adept at some discourse of science of the North Atlantic of relevance to the ex-colonial/neo-colonial world and its inhabitants, but a point of departure is crucial and vital where the anti-science of liberation intervenes towards the completion of the process of liberation. To fail to have a potent point of departure means the reliance on white supremacist discourse to effect liberation from itself, or naming the KKK as an instrument of liberation of non-whites from the hegemony of white supremacist discourse. An exercise in futility driven by a sophist discourse.

Chapter 5

A Discourse of Colonial Domination Deconstructed

Extreme Ambivalence

In chapter 4 of Fanon's work he presents a deconstruction of the book "Prospero and Caliban: Psychology of Colonisation" by M. Mannoni on the nature of the relations between coloniser and colonised. Fanon states: "Having lived under the extreme ambivalence inherent in the colonial situation, M. Mannoni has managed to achieve a grasp-unfortunately too exhaustive-of the psychological phenomena that govern the relations between coloniser and colonised." (Fanon 1977 pg. 83). Fanon insists that colonial domination generates extreme ambivalence expressed in the nature of human action of the colonised. Has this extreme ambivalence disappeared with constitutional decolonisation and independence from the colonial overlord? The most potent expression of this extreme ambivalence is the duality of the love, the desire for whiteness and the lust for the white woman combined with the hatred, even the racist hatred of the white man. But the concept of ambivalence is a crafted discursive weapon utilised against non-white peoples towards ensuring sustainable white hegemony. All Native/First Peoples who made first contact with the white man can attest to the deliberate strategy of lies and deception conveyed via white languages to facilitate and ensure the sustainable success of white hegemony. But in this reality the white man is never described as being ambivalent as they express values, mores and normalising instruments by which to dominate what they simply abhor, don't believe in; and they go to the extent of constructing political discourses driven by these values, mores and normalising instruments that they simply don't believe in. In the exercise of power what they do believe in is revealed and it is not the rule of law and the constitution, but they are never ambivalent for ambivalence is a condition of action reserved for non-white people. This discursive concept is a weapon of colonisation.

Real Coordinates of the Colonial Situation

Fanon continues: "I propose to show that, although he has devoted 225 pages to the study of the colonial situation, M. Mannoni has not understood its real coordinates. When one approaches a problem as that of taking inventory of the possibilities for understanding between two different peoples, one should be doubly careful." (Fanon 1977 pg. 84). Fanon insists that Mannoni's study fails to understand, therefore reveal the real coordinates of colonial domination. Fanon states that Mannoni's fundamental theme is that the colonial situation is the result of confrontation between civilised men and primitive men which creates a special situation from which emerges illusions and misunderstandings that only a psychological analysis can unravel. Mannoni is then an apologist for white colonial imperialism seen in his position, for Fanon, where he insists that the inferiority complex of the colonised predated colonial domination and racism does not reflect an economic structure. Fanon makes his position clear on his approach in this work as follows: "A given society is racist or it is not. Statements, for example, that the north of France is more racist than the south, that racism is the work of underlings and hence in no way involves the ruling class, that France is one of the least racist countries in the world are the product of men incapable of straight thinking." (Fanon 1977 pg. 85). Attempts to create shades of racism, or more or less racist is simply an attempt to mask realities of racism and the social order and to give potency to a discourse of power. Fanon rejects this position. Fanon continues: "I hope I may be forgiven for asking that those that take it on themselves to describe colonialism remember one thing: that it is utopian to try to ascertain in what ways one kind of inhuman behaviour differs from another kind of inhuman behaviour." (Fanon 1977 pg. 86). Comparisons to create a hierarchy of brutality which insists that all brutality is not the same, some are more brutal than others as seen in the hierarchy of West Indian enslavement where you have the position that you did have a spectrum of enslavement with humane enslavement existing in specific islands. Fanon now states his purpose in this work: "In this work I have made it a point to convey the misery of the black man. Physically and affectively. I have not wished to be objective. Besides, that would be dishonest: It is not possible for me to be objective. Is there in truth any difference between one racism and another? Do not all of them show the same collapse, the same bankruptcy of man? (Fanon 1977 pg. 86). To be objective as defined by the white man's science is to defeat Fanon's purpose driving his mission expressed in the completed work under study. This objectivity mutes the expression of the pain, the angst racism dumps on the colonised whilst rendering sterile and stillborn projects launched to realise the liberation project as real. The base position is that pain, oppression and arrested development must be articulated and to do this the white man's objectivity has to be abandoned and with it the attempt to victimise us for our oppression at the hands of the dominant.

Racist Structure, the Collective Unconscious, the bad Nigger

Fanon notes the position of Mannoni on racist, apartheid South Africa with reference to Mannoni's denial of an economic aspect to racism. Fanon states: "M. Mannoni believes that the contempt of the poor whites of South Africa for the Negro has nothing to do with economic factors." "we could point out to M. Mannoni that the displacement of the white proletariat's aggression on to the black proletariat is fundamentally a result of the economic structure of South Africa. What is South Africa? A boiler in which thirteen million blacks are clubbed and penned in by two and a half million whites. If the poor whites hate the Negroes, it is not, as M. Mannoni would have us believe, because 'racialism is the work of petty officials, small traders, and colonials who have toiled much without great success.' No; it is because the structure of South Africa is a racist structure." (Fanon 1977 pgs.86-87). Fanon cites the faulty analysis of Mannoni with reference to apartheid South Africa. Mannoni posits his apologist argument which masks the racist social order of South Africa by insisting that racism is the instrument of the lower levels of white South African society illustrated by the hatred of the poor whites for the Africans. Fanon insists that racism in South Africa is not the preserve of the lower levels of white society as the South African social order is structured on racism where race and class are joined ensuring that racism and a racist social order impacts the economic order and the class structure. White workers must earn more than African workers for the same tasks done, African workers must never be placed in positions of power over white workers and they must be segregated in the workplace as in the wider society. In apartheid South Africa racism trumps the supposed rationality of capitalism. Racism is at the same time a mechanism to enable super exploitation of African workers whilst it rewards the white worker as the master race of the working class. Fanon continues: "All forms of exploitation are identical because all of them are applied against the same 'object': man." "Colonial racism is no different from any other racism." (Fanon 1977 pg. 88). To differentiate between racisms and exploitations is for Fanon an attempt to evade and mask reality by the apologists. Fanon returns to South Africa as follows: "I said just above that South Africa has a racist structure. Now I shall go further and say that Europe has a racist structure. It is plain to see that M. Mannoni has no interest in this problem, for he says, 'France is unquestionably one of the least racialist-minded countries in the world.' Be glad that you are French, my fine Negro friends, even if it is a little hard, for your counterparts in America are much worse off than you...France is a racist country, for the myth of the bad nigger is part of the collective unconscious." (Fanon 1977 pg. 92). Fanon now presents Mannoni's method of differentiating between degrees of racism in an attempt to create typologies of racist countries thereby creating the basis of his apologetics where France is bad but not as bad as others thereby insisting that there are racist countries with silver linings which are preferable to those with none. Fanon posits his definition of a racist country as one in which the myth of the bad nigger is present in the collective unconscious thereby presenting two concepts demanding definition.

Colonial Inferiority Complex

Fanon next deals with Mannoni's position on the colonial inferiority complex. Fanon states: "The feelings of inferiority of the colonised is the correlative to the European's feeling of superiority. Let us have the courage to say it outright. *It is the racist who creates his inferior.*" (Fanon 1977 pg. 93). Fanon states his position that European hegemony constitutes the inferiority of those dominated in colonial power relations. Fanon then indicates that Mannoni holds an entirely different position when he insists that the inferiority of the colonised is the artifice created by the colonised to deal with the loss of her/his dependency on the European coloniser. Fanon states: "To the extent to which M. Mannoni's real typical Malagasy takes on 'dependent behaviour,' all is for the best; if, however, he forgets his place, if he takes it into his head to be the equal of the European, then the said European is indignant and casts out the upstart-who, in such circumstances, in this 'exceptional case,' pays for his own rejection of dependence with an inferiority complex." (Fanon 1977 pg.

93). To reap the full benefit of French domination the Malagasy must become dependent on the coloniser for it is only via this dominant/subordinate, white/black dynamic will the benefit of being dominated accrue to the colonised. Mannoni is then unapologetically insisting that the French are the master race and all paths to development must commence from black dependency. At some point in time the dependent now adopts the invalid position that she/he is now equal to the French coloniser, the master race and is cut off from the subservient flow with the French coloniser. In response to this loss of presence, this flow of grace from the master race, the cast out Negro develops an inferiority complex. Mannoni's discourse is blatantly racist to its core, in fact it is white supremacist for all development can only come from the master race, all non-white races cannot generate this development independently, in order to tap into the grace of the master race all non-white races must willingly submit, be dependent, be submissive to the master race and those who reject this servile position will be excised and revert to their inferior selves but this time burdened with a brave inferiority complex having tasted of white development and civilisation. This is simply a discourse of power formulated to seduce the non-whites of the world to be pliant and servile in the face of white domination.

Bilateral Totality

In his continuing critique of Mannoni's analysis of the Malagasy under French colonial domination Fanon states: *"After having sealed the Malagasy into his own customs, after having evolved a unilateral analysis of his view of the world, after having described the Malagasy within a closed circle, after having noted that the Malagasy has a dependency relation toward his ancestors-a strong tribal characteristic-M. Mannoni, in defiance of all objectivity, applies his conclusions to a bilateral totality-deliberately ignoring the fact that, since Gallieni, the Malagasy has ceased to exist."* (Fanon 1977 pg. 94). Mannoni focuses on the anthropology and psychology of the Malagasy with no reference to the reality of French colonial domination of Madagascar. A unilateral analysis focused on the native applied to a bilateral totality of colonial domination where Mannoni constructs a profile of the Malagasy before French colonial domination and projects it into the colonial era as the genesis for the condition of the colonised under French colonial domination. Mannoni is then more than an apologist for colonial domination, he is in fact a discursive agent manufacturing a scientific discourse that attempts to mask the reality of French colonial domination in Madagascar. This is especially so for Fanon as he insists that Mannoni has erased the historical fact that the French conquered Madagascar by force, thereby erasing the Malagasy that existed before the colonial conquest, therefore the precolonial Malagasy Mannoni constructs is irrelevant, a mask, a slight of hand trick by Mannoni. Fanon describes colonial domination as a bilateral totality with two sides locked in a dynamic, coloniser and colonised placed in a space that is a totality, a whole, a wholeness, a complete operational terrain which impacts all sides situated in this space. In the North Atlantic a totality is conceived as an organic whole with its needs which surpasses that of the sum total of those of its inmates. What is to be determined is if Fanon is using the concept in this manner. What is already noted in the deconstruction of the work thus far is Fanon's position that the colonial totality impacts both colonised and colonised but not equally given the black-white complex. Fanon continues his critique of Mannoni's position on the Malagasy as follows: "What we wanted from M. Mannoni was an explanation of the colonial situation. He notably overlooked providing it." (Fanon 1977 pg. 94). Fanon continues: "What M. Mannoni has forgotten is that the Malagasy alone no longer exists; he has forgotten that the Malagasy *exists with the European*. The arrival of the white man in Madagascar shattered not only its horizons but its psychological mechanisms. As everyone has pointed out, alterity for the black man is not the black but the white man." (Fanon 1977 pgs. 96-97). For Fanon, Mannoni failed to provide an analysis of the colonial domination of Madagascar and its impact on the Native. Mannoni's unilateral focus on the Native cannot provide an analysis of colonial domination as colonial domination is bilateral never unilateral as the Malagasy exists, shares space with the European in a power relation. Fanon then gives an insight into his totality having horizons and psychological mechanisms where the French colonial conqueror destroys the horizons and psychological mechanisms of the Malagasy and put in place colonial horizons and psychological mechanisms to ensure the subservience of the Native and the hegemony of the coloniser.

Hallucinatory Whitening

Fanon presents his position on the unconscious of the colonised gathered through the use of psychoanalysis to interpret dreams. After hearing and analysing the dream of a black patient Fanon presents his analysis as follows: "1. My patient is suffering from an inferiority complex. His psychic structure is in danger of disintegration. 2, If he is overwhelmed to such a degree by his wish to be white, it is because he lives in a society that makes his inferiority complex possible. In a society that derives its stability from the perpetuation of this complex, in a society that proclaims the superiority of one race; to the identical degree to which that society creates difficulties for him, he will find himself thrust into a neurotic situation." "As a psychoanalyst, I should help my patient to become conscious of his unconscious and abandon his attempts at a hallucinatory whitening, but also to act in the direction of a change in the social structure." (Fanon 1977 pg. 100). Fanon's diagnosis is: 1. His black patient has an inferiority complex which is potent enough to deconstruct his psychic structure. 2. His patient is swamped by the drive, the desire to be white and the potency of his inferior complex, his desire to be white is as a direct result of the nature of the society he inhabits. A social order that demands his inferiority complex as a necessity to its stability and sustainable order. A racist society, a white supremacist racist society that assaults his black self and presents hurdles in his path as a human undertaking life's journey. The patient responds by being neurotic especially enhanced and illustrated by his hallucinatory whitening. Fanon releases his concept of hallucinatory whitening in this context which describes the solution adopted by the black patient to the racist assault on his black persona by whitening his worldview and concept of self but this whitening is hallucinatory for only the black patient sees himself as white. The black patient's whiteness exists in only his mind with its perception mechanism for white society and his fellow blacks can see him only as black. The black man's whiteness is then a painful hallucination which brings no benefit to him, only harm. Fanon then prescribes that his patient must first become conscious of the nature and condition of his unconscious, move to abandon his drive for hallucinatory whiteness and most important of all understand and act upon the understanding that liberation from the inferiority complex and being neurotic is not possible without the dismantling of the racist social structure. Liberation demands revolutionary action, for the action of revolution, the pursuit of revolution cleanses the unconscious of the inferiority complex and its neuroses. Fanon with this section of his text presents his position that revolutionary violence is a cleansing force. Fanon continues: "In other words, the black man should no longer be confronted by the dilemma, *turn white or disappear*; but he should be able to take cognizance of the possibility of existence." "my objective, once his motivations have been brought into consciousness, will be to put him in a position to *choose* action (or passivity) with respect to the real source of the conflict-that is, toward the social structures." (Fanon 1977 pg. 100). Revolutionary psychoanalysis has to point to the pathway that ends the desire that conjures up the iron clad choice of whitening or disappearance to now visualise black existence as being realisable, possible real. Fanon's objective is to attain success in changing his patient's motivational structure is to present him with a new existential choice which targets the social structure with the choice of action to change the social structure/revolutionary action situated in a revolutionary praxis and the choice of passivity. This then is Fanon's revolutionary praxis in his own words.

The Racial Distribution of Guilt

Fanon now grapples with black on black racism where non-white races unleash race hate on each other thereby dividing the races in the face of white hegemony. Fanon was impacted by this potent black on black race hate and in the work is stating his explanation for it as it is potent amongst non-white races colonised by whites. Fanon states: "The Frenchman does not like the Jew, who does not like the Arab, who does not like the Negro...The Arab is told: 'If you are poor, it is because the Jew has bled you and taken everything from you.' The Jew is told: 'You are not of the same class as the Arab because you are really white and because you have Einstein and Bergson.' The Negro is told: 'You are the best soldiers in the French Empire; the Arabs think they are better than you, but they are wrong.' But that is not true; the Negro is told nothing because no one has anything to tell him, the Senegalese trooper, the good-soldier-under-command, the brave-fellow-who-only-knows-how-to-obey." "Unable to stand up to all the demands, the white man sloughs off his responsibilities. I have a name for this: the racial distribution of guilt." (Fanon 1977 pg. 103). The traditional explanation for the scenario described by Fanon is the colonial divide and conquer strategy. But in order for the strategy to work, to be effective the product of the black-white complex must be operationally manifest amongst the subservient races and those races sharing common space with the white man exercising hegemony must have reason to utilise white on black race hate against each other. This reason is only found in the economic power relations of the social order where these non-white races are in competition with each other for economic space and power which adopts political expression and impacts the political order including the drive for the post-colonial order. These non-white races have then political power relations that are expressed via the racist mechanism that the whites exerting hegemony have unleashed on all races in the space and their domination of the economic space has ensured its use by the non-white races. The white man has then unleashed the jinn from the bottle and is intent on distributing the guilt generated by his hegemony to all the non-white races under his hegemony. For all the inmates of the space drink at the poisoned well of race hate, and are equally guilty of race hate, and with the departure of the colonial massa this well will continue to be drunk from ensuring and affirming the legacy of massa which is used as the abrogation of the guilt of the white man with racist arrogance and hubris presently in the 21st century North Atlantic. Black on black race hate then allows the white man to escape the demands made upon them as a result of their actions. This escape hatch has now evolved in the 21st century into the open door that enables and justifies the call for racist exclusivism in the face of the threat posed by non-white invaders of the citadel of white culture and history. But in the examples of black on black racism used by Fanon he insists that the discourse to the Senegalese is a lie for the Negro is the archetype enemy, the common threat and the common repository of hate shared by all races within the space. But the Senegalese is just a trooper nothing more or less, a pliant, armed, brave trooper under white command feared by all races of the space, as a result the strategy applied to him to ensure sustainable compliance is silence, for to politicise the Senegalese trooper is a pathway fraught with danger. To remain the feared, obedient shock trooper of the French Empire the Senegalese must be excluded from this discourse to ensure he remains the invoker of nightmares that afflict the colonised Malagasy. This is also why when the Arabs are in revolt the French used their non-white troops to supress these revolts to invoke nightmares driven by fear of the black troops that drives black on black racism and racial guilt distribution. Fanon states: "If those good-for-nothings, the Arabs, took it into their heads to revolt, it was not in the name of any acceptable principle but purely and simply in order to get rid of their '*bicot*' unconscious." (Fanon 1977 pg. 103). The use of black troops against Arab anticolonial revolts allowed the white man to dismiss the revolt as a violent clash between different non-white races driven by black on black race hate or Arab versus bicot/jigaboo/nigger/African. Having distributed his race guilt, the white man is now claiming innocence as it was not an Arab rebellion against white colonial domination but a black on black race war against bicots. Or as in the 21st century, where they are claiming the absence of, even the nonexistence of guilt for in their treatment of non-white races, from the past to the present, guilt simply does not arise for it's a matter of manifest destiny and race preservation. You have then to place the slave trader and all the expressions of colonial imperialism in their historical context where all their actions were normal for that era hence no guilt is assumed nor accepted. Which then insists that no guilt is assumed nor accepted for racist actions in the 21st century, for they are normal for this era of the grave threat to the white homelands by non-white races, simply National Socialism with a 21st century veneer.

Colonial Trauma and the Individual

With reference to the interpretation of the dreams of the colonised Malagasy specifically those involving the Senegalese shock troops. Fanon states: "since we know what the archetype of the Senegalese can represent for the Malagasy, the discoveries of Freud are of no use to us here. What must be done is to restore this dream *to its proper time*, and this time is the period during which eighty thousand natives were killed-that is to say, one of every fifty persons in the population; and to *its proper place*, and this place is an island of four million people, at the centre of which no real relationship can be established, where dissension breaks out in every direction, where the only masters are lies and demagogy. One must concede that in some circumstances the *socius* is more important than the individual." (Fanon 1977 pgs. 104-105). The dream is rooted in the slaughter of the Malagasies at the hands of the French imperialist invaders and their use of their Senegalese shock troops. Fanon insists that the trauma of the slaughter and its diagnosis renders Freud's psychoanalysis irrelevant to this task therefore its use can only result in misdiagnosis and damage to the patients it was applied to. Fanon comes to the conclusion that in specific cases the causative realities of the social order, the bonds common to a social order outstrip the causative reality rooted in the individual. The psychiatrist, the psychoanalyst must then be able to discern when the socius outstrips the individual and accepts and acts on this reality.

Mannoni's Discourse

Fanon ends the chapter by debunking M. Mannoni's concept of the Prospero complex that afflicts the white coloniser with the colonised as Caliban. Fanon states: "If one adds that many Europeans go to the colonies because it is possible for them to grow rich quickly there, that with rare exceptions the colonial is a merchant, or rather a trafficker, one will have grasped the psychology of the man who arouses in the autochthonous population 'the feeling of inferiority.'" (Fanon 1977 pg. 108). The nature of the social order then impacts the coloniser and the colonised for the white carpetbaggers that descend on the colonies in their quest for quick wealth are in no way paragons of the inherently superior white race supposedly vitally necessary to sustainable white hegemony over non-white peoples. There is then a missing dimension to the operational mechanics of colonial power relations that Mannoni simply cannot see as his perceptive paradigm is deeply flawed. Fanon continues: "As for the Malagasy 'dependency complex,' at least in the only form in which we can reach it and analyse it, it too proceeds from the arrival of white colonisers on the island." (Fanon 1977 pg. 108). Mannoni's Malagasy dependency complex has serious heuristic problems with the only discernible form being the product of colonial domination which contradicts Mannoni's position. "From its other form, from this original complex in its pure state that supposedly characterised the Malagasy mentality throughout the whole precolonial period, it appears to me that M. Mannoni lacks the slightest basis on which to ground any conclusion applicable to the situation, the problems, or the potentialities of the Malagasy in the present time." (Fanon 1977 pg.108). Mannoni's core concept is the precolonial dependency complex of the Malagasy but the concept has no relevance to the present reality of colonised Madagascar as an effective analytical tool, for it is a concept destined to mask the reality of colonial domination by insisting that the problem of the colonised Malagasy is the creation of the Malagasy in their precolonial past. Mannoni has written not an apologetic for colonial domination but a scientific analysis that denies the destructive impact of French colonial domination on Madagascar laying all the blame for Malagasy arrested development on the Malagasy themselves. Mannoni is thereby positing that French colonial development was the only and necessary path to modernity and development but their precolonial psychological mal-development blocked their access to the modernity and development on offer from French colonial development. At this point Mannoni's work exposes its task as a justification for French colonial domination.

Chapter 6
White Being, Ontology and Black Certain-Uncertainty

Unattainable Ontology

In chapter five of the work being analysed Fanon delves deeply and incisively into the nature of black being. Fanon states: "and then I found that I was an object in the midst of other objects. Sealed into that crushing objecthood," (Fanon 1977 pg. 109). "As long as the black man is among his own, he will have no occasion, except in minor internal conflicts, to experience his being through others." (Fanon 1977 pg. 108). "but every ontology is made unattainable in a colonised and civilised society." (Fanon 1977 pg. 108). When black is attached to being to designate a different type of being, the being of the other, the black human becomes trapped in objecthood where the manufactured soul of colonial domination envelops the non-white and constitutes the being of the non-white, the nigger, chink, wet back etc. This instrument of white hegemony crushes the being of the non-white with an all-encompassing objecthood to the point where the non-white has to experience the being allocated to them through the white man's being. In this reality the non-white being has no ontology for the ontology of the white man's artifice attached to his body is the white man's ontology and the non-white can never articulate the white man's ontology attached to his being for it is not his, whilst his alternative ontology is under constant assault, a silenced discourse. The attached ontology of white hegemony is then an unattainable ontology whilst the alternate ontology is a silenced ontology, the dynamic of which constitutes the crushing objecthood. Fanon continues: "In the Weltanschauung of the colonised people there is an impurity, a flaw that outlaws any ontological explanation. Ontology-once it is finally admitted as leaving existence by the wayside-does not permit us to understand the being of the black man. For not only must the black man be black; he must be black in relation to the white man. The black man has no ontological resistance in the eyes of the white man." (Fanon 1977 pg. 110). Ontology is a white concept that simply cannot apply to the nature of being of a colonised black man as the ontology of a black is a contrived artifice, just as the black soul that envelops the non-white body is necessary to sustainable white hegemony. With reference to the white man the non-white can only be black which is an expression of the black soul that envelops the non-white body and the manufactured ontology attached to the black soul that inundates the non-white body with white being and nothingness. A black man that embraces this white ontology of the black soul can offer no ontological resistance to the hegemonic white man, all that can be proffered is servility and surrender. The end result is a black worldview that is faulty, flawed, servile and obedient, devoid of an independent ontology capable of resistance, self-definition and self-determination hence liberation.

Body, Certain-Uncertainty

Fanon continues on the issue of body, being and consciousness as follows: "The black man among his own in the twentieth century does not know at what moment his inferiority complex comes into being through the other." "And then the occasion arose when I had to meet the white man's eyes. An unfamiliar weight burdened me. The real world challenged my claims. In the white world the man of colour encounters difficulties in the development of his bodily schema. Consciousness of the body is solely a negating activity. It is a third-person consciousness. The body is surrounded by an atmosphere of certain-uncertainty." (Fanon 1977 pgs. 110-111). The problematic of the consciousness of the black body for Fanon became readily apparent in spaces dominated by the white race where the black body was inferior to the epitome that is the white body and its ontology of being. The problematic expresses itself in the programme to alter by whatever means the black body chemically, by attached additions or implants and ultimately surgically. This is also expressed in a consciousness that is received, passive, dependent where self is defined externally and implanted on the black body constituting a third-person consciousness. This servile, constituted consciousness must negate specific activity in its recipient whilst it ensures white hegemony. Such a consciousness generates an operational netherworld for the black man driven by certain-uncertainty where only uncertainty is certain as consciousness is constituted to serve white hegemony. The advance of digital technology, which has enabled the globalisation of white hegemonic discourse on a real time basis, has facilitated in the 21st century the impact of certain-uncertainty in Asia and Africa illustrated by the adherence to normalising mechanisms of power that problematize the non-white body and the strategies adopted to modify the non-white body as skin lightening creams and surgical procedures to implant copies of desirous supposedly white lips, noses and eyelids on non-white bodies. In the 21st century certain-uncertainty is at its most lethally potent since this mechanism of power was constituted by white racist discourse.

A Historico-Racial Schema

Fanon now insists that this certain-uncertainty is the product of a historico-racial schema by which to attain and ensure sustainable white hegemony by constituting the Negro to enable sustainable white hegemony. Fanon states: "and embarked on researches that might make it possible for the miserable Negro to whiten himself and thus to throw off the burden of that corporeal malediction. Below the corporeal schema I had sketched a historico-racial schema. The elements that I used had been provided for me...by the other, the white man, who had woven me out of a thousand details, anecdotes, stories." (Fanon 1977 pg. 111). The black body conjures up the need and quest for whiteness in an attempt to erase the corporeal malediction posed by the black body but Fanon discovers that the quest for whiteness, as is the corporeal malediction, are the products of a historico-racial schema. An overarching strategy that spans history with a racist schema operationalised through constituting the Negro. Fanon was then using tools to unearth the historico-racial schema supplied by the white man as Fanon himself was the constituted product of the historico-racial schema of the hegemonic white man. Fanon was then living the state of certain-uncertainty a circular dance between the historico-schema and personal lived experience which masks the reality that we are constituted by white hegemonic mechanisms of power. Fanon continues by insisting that the cement of the matrix is *historicity* for it is the depth, the continuity and above all the expression of the concept of white supremacist time and epoch thereby framing the white racial schema and its mechanisms of power.

The Racial Epidermal Schema

Fanon states: "Then, assailed at various points, the corporeal schema crumbled, its place taken by a racial epidermal schema. In the train it was no longer a question of being aware of my body in the third person but in a triple person. In the train I was given not one but two, three places...I existed triply." (Fanon 1977 pg. 112). The corporeal schema falls apart revealing the driving force of the historico-racial schema which is the epidermalisation of non-whites where a hierarchy is established that stretches from the apex of white and pure as driven snow to the despised base of the darkest black, synonymous with evil, physical and sexual potency visualised as threats to the white man by targeting the white woman with a range of intermediary shades that range from black to white and from white to black. The entire epidermal schema is racist and it defines and frames human interaction, perceptions and transactions as a racist process. This hierarchy enables the white man to classify every human of non-white origin into a classificatory space in this hierarchy, which constitutes this person so classified generating white expectations of their behaviour. Non-white persons classified in this hierarchy will have specific instruments of power applied to normalise their behaviour on an ongoing basis. This racial epidermal schema constitutes hierarchies that reflect the immediate reality of engagement with non-white peoples for the sets of non-whites to deal with vary by epidermal colour demanding fluid hierarchies. A single black person moving through multiple epidermal colour hierarchies will encounter multiple hierarchies, orders and instruments of normalisation and must be able to respond to multiple hierarchies, their order and power relations. A non-white has then to operationalise multiple perceptions of multiple hierarchies and their demands thereof in order to survive and to be able to respond adequately to the fluidity of these hierarchies in their operational mode. All non-white people must have multioperational perceptive abilities driven by the impact of multiple truths for our reality is hinged on power relations defined by the racist hierarchy of skin colour. To survive functionally whilst traversing this netherworld where our places in the hierarchy and the expectations thereof are always fluid at the caprice of the white man we must then be functionally schizophrenic. The racial-epidermal schema is then the mechanism of power that drives the relational reality of the black-white complex. Long before I learnt to read and write I learnt the nature of the multiple hierarchies of colour where my colour determined my position in the hierarchy which changed dramatically according to the colour composition of the group I found myself in. I was always told that I was superior to the persons whose skins were darker than mine and I was expected to behave as a superior white man with these groups. But when I found myself in a group with my white cousins my white grandfather made it clear to me that I am placed below those white cousins but still placed above the blacks. What was allocated to the whites I was denied but would enjoy more than what was allocated to blacks and I was expected to accept this position, exalt the white man and hate the black man with all my being. I was then expected to desire and pursue whiteness but its pursuit was possible for me as I carried the necessary genetic code. Then there are the hierarchies you find yourself in with black people where you are viewed as something not black. To survive a racist terrain, you are then called upon to be functionally schizophrenic. In this terrain power relations are defined and driven by the racial-epidermal schema.

Fanon describes the product of the racial epidermal-schema as follows: "I was responsible at the same time for my body, for my race, for my ancestors. I subjected myself to an objective examination, I discovered my blackness, my ethnic characteristics; and I was battered down by tom-toms, cannibalism, intellectual deficiency, fetishism, racial defects, slave-ships, and above all else, above all: 'Sho good eatin.' On that day, completely dislocated, unable to be abroad with the other, the white man, who unmercifully imprisoned me, I took myself far off from my own presence, far indeed, and made myself an object." (Fanon 1977 pg. 112). Fanon discovers all that is his legacy as a member of his race but he faces the assault of the racial epidermal schema where he is jigaboo, the souls manufactured by the white man through which the white man not only assaults Fanon to normalise him but through which the white man normalises himself ensuring the sustainability of the racial epidermal schema across time and epoch. Fanon then in reaction to this sustained assault surrendered by making himself an object by accepting objecthood. The individual under the assault of the normalising instrument of white power must execute the act of their surrender by making themselves an object. This is then an act of suicide, of self-immolation where you render yourself into a zombie. Fanon states: "My body was given back to me sprawled out, distorted, recoloured, clad in mourning in that white winter day." (Fanon 1977 pg.113). Fanon after making himself an object became a zombie but the hierarchy of colour and exclusion is not modified to reward zombie objecthood for the racist epidermal schema must police exclusion in a bid to be sustainable. Fanon states: "The white world, the only honourable one, barred me from all participation. A man was supposed to behave like a man. I was expected to behave as a black man-or at least like a nigger." (Fanon 1977 pg. 114). You are not a man for long as you are non-white you are expected to be normalised in keeping with the white man's norm that defines what we are. The only man is the white man, the only normal man is the white man and the only normalising man is the white man. This exclusionary prescription is the product of the operationalisation of the racial epidermal schema. Fanon states: "I resolved, since it was impossible for me to get away from an *inborn complex*, to assert myself as a BLACK MAN." (Fanon 1977 pg. 115). It is impossible to evade the inborn complex which leaves the only open path to adopt the norm of the Black Man constituted by the white man's racial epidermal schema. At this stage Fanon is deepening his objecthood. Fanon continues on this theme: "But in my case everything takes on a *new* guise. I am given no chance; I am overdetermined from without. I am the slave not of the 'idea' that others have of me but of my own appearance." "I progress by crawling. And already I am being dissected under white eyes, the only real eyes. I am *fixed*." "When people like me, they tell me it is in spite of my colour. When they dislike me, they point out that it is not because of my colour. Either way, I am locked into the infernal circle." (Fanon 1977 pg. 116). The white norm of the black man then traps the black in an epidermal jail, a singularity of race norms policing a social order where the epidermal nature of the black is overdetermined from without by power external of him, white racist power which anchors her/him to a specific slot in the epidermal hierarchy of skin colour in all its visible symbolic manifestations for the life of the non-white. Hence the drive to alter the colour, to change the appearance, and ultimately to wash the genetic code. Fanon continues: "My blackness was there, dark and unarguable. And it tormented me, pursued me, disturbed me, angered me. There was a myth of the Negro that had to be destroyed at all costs." (Fanon 1977 pg. 117). His blackness defined and placed on him by the epidermal schema in its policing of the black constitutes a netherworld that encapsulates the black.

What then is my experience with the epidermal schema? The condition of certain-uncertainty is real where I am expected to hate all people with a white racist hate whose skins are darker than mine whilst simultaneously accepting and acting upon my inferiority as I am less than white. Driven by self-hate I must hate all persons darker than myself whilst loving and adoring the inherently superior master race, willing accepting servility, subservience and permanently acting on a desire for whiteness. I was called upon to accept and answer to, to mould my life by the descriptive condition attached to my skin by my white family: mongrel. I was not white enough, not Chinese enough, not black enough to facilitate an easy journey through the various hierarchies of the epidermal schema I transitioned on a daily basis where I then became an enigma in an epidermal schema that demands classificatory probity and permanence. I then turned my enigmatic condition to that of rebellion when I learned that persons as myself pose a grave threat to the sustainability of the epidermal schema, especially those of us who reject the racist worldview of the schema. For posing such a threat you pay a grave price which persuades those as myself to be expressions of the most potent purveyors of self-hate expressed via rabid, paranoid black on black racism where you attack yourself via the attack on the other's other. You are the servile, subservient, active, rabid racist without reward and acceptance from the master race served. What are you then but mentally ill!

Fanon continues on the theme on the nature of the racist epidermal schema as follows: "I had read it rightly. It was hate; I was hated, despised, detested...by an entire race. I was against something unreasoned. I would personally say that for a man whose only weapon is reason there is nothing more neurotic than unreason." (Fanon 1977 pg. 118). Racism applied to human action and interaction constitutes an operational reality when viewed via the perspective of reason is simply neurotic unreason which must impact the humans caught up in these orders of actions and interactions. Fanon states: "There will always will be a world-a white world-between you and us...The other's total inability to liquidate the past once and for all." (Fanon 1977 pg. 122). The white man will always constitute his white world that separates white from non-white creating the white man's comfort zone. The issue is then its hegemony for this is what drives the refusal of the white man to erase his past for it defines and justifies his hegemony, the need for racism and its spatial expression. Fanon continues: "I had rationalised the world and the world had rejected me on the basis of colour prejudice. Since no agreement was possible on the level of reason. I threw myself back toward unreason. It was up to the white man to be more irrational than I. Out of the necessitates of my struggle I had chosen the method of regression, but the fact remains that it was an unfamiliar weapon; here I am at home; I am made of the irrational; I wade in the irrational." "From the opposite end of the white world a magical Negro culture was hailing me. Negro sculpture! I began to flush with pride. Was this our salvation?" (Fanon 1977 pg. 123). Fanon's skin was the basis of his rejection by the white world as there was no merit in reason and rationality even though they are white discursive constructs, for the exclusionary space defined by the epidermal schema is strategically vital and central to white hegemony. Fanon then returns to unreason and irrationality but the white man outstrips Fanon's irrationality and is always capable of outstripping the irrationality of the non-whites driven by the fear of a black planet. Fanon then becomes an expression of irrationality as his worldview is irrational seen in his vision of a magical Negro culture created in the womb of the white man's world of the epidermal schema. His irrationality can envisage salvation forthcoming from the same womb as the epidermal schema, irrationality, lunacy or both?

Fanon's Philosophical Discourse

In the chapter under analysis Fanon now presents his full blown philosophical discourse framed in poetic lyricism. Fanon the philosopher states: "I walk on white nails. Sheets of water threaten my soul on fire. Face to face with these rites, I am doubly alert." "Yes, we are-we Negroes-backward, simple, free in our behaviour. That is because for us the body is not something opposed to what you call the mind. We are in the world. And long live the couple. Man and Earth!" "The white man wants the world; he wants it for himself alone. He finds himself predestined master of this world. He enslaves it. An acquisitive relation is established between the world and him. But there exist other values that fit only my forms. Like a magician, I robbed the white man of 'a certain world,' forever after lost to him and his." "Between the world and me a relation of coexistence was established. I had discovered the primeval One. My 'speaking hands' tore at the hysterical throat of the world." (Fanon 1977 pgs. 126-128). The Negro and the white man are locked in a dynamic, a dance of mutually irreconcilable opposites in spite of the hegemony of the white man for there is always resistance to power as power begets resistance. The white man is the hegemonic entity that commands the world and his being is alienated from the world as a result of this hegemony. The Negro as the other hand robs the white man of this other, certain world as the white man in his desire for hegemony must be denied this other, certain world such is the cost of racist hegemony. But the hegemonic white man insists that this certain world is the constructed fantasy of conquered races unsubstantiated by his vaunted science and the abiding hegemonic reality is that in spite of having a relation of coexistence with the world and finding the primeval one, you walk on white nails and under ever present threat of having your soul on fire extinguished. In the exercise of hegemonic power, the white man can and will destroy Man and Earth simply just be aware of the 21st century.

Fanon returns to his self-analysis as follows: "the white man explained to me that, genetically, I represented a stage of development. Then I had the feeling that I was repeating a cycle. My originality had been torn out of me. But I was haunted by a galaxy of erosive stereotypes: The Negro's *sui generis* odour...the Negro's *sui generis* good nature...the Negro's *sui generis* gullibility." (Fanon 1977 pg. 129). The assault on the other is unrelenting as the other is different in a manner and with a nature that presents a threat to the hegemony of the white man. The assault must then relentlessly attack originality, essence and worldview to normalise the difference by replacing them with the black soul. Fanon states: "I tested the limits of my essence; beyond all doubt there was not much of it left. It was here that I made my most remarkable discovery. Properly speaking, this discovery was a rediscovery. The white man was wrong, I was not a primitive, not even a half-man." (Fanon 1977 pg. 130). To counter the ravages of the racist assault there then must be a rediscovery of the existential condition before colonial domination that is in opposition to the discourse of white supremacy. But what is the efficacy of this rediscovery in the face of the concerted assault that transcends time and geopolitics? Fanon states: "I made a complete audit of my ailment. I wanted to be typically Negro-it was no longer possible. I wanted to be white-that was a joke. And, when I tried, on the level of ideas and intellectual activity, to reclaim my negritude, it was snatched away from me." (Fanon 1977 pg. 132). Fanon can no longer be a typical Negro nor can he be white and at the level of the idea there is no negritude to reclaim which raises the question if negritude, the condition of being the typical negro and the desire for whiteness are all instruments of white power to ensure sustainable white hegemony? For we must make ourselves objects! All conceptions of discursive resistance formulated under the era of white sustainable hegemony utilising the language and paradigm of white hegemony carries within itself the traps and pitfalls of meaning to destroy the drive for liberation. The white man's language is his and was framed by his discourses to serve his hegemony which necessitates that we must first deconstruct and neuter his language to serve us. Fanon continues: "but he forgot that this negativity draws its worth from an almost substantive absoluteness." (Fanon 1977 pg. 134). The negativity that drives the white racist hegemonic assault on non-white races is grounded in and sustained by the absolute of the inherent superiority of the white race expressed via various discursive concepts as manifest destiny, rights of conquest, eugenics and the Final Solution. This negativity fed by an absolute then ensures the rapid, paranoid, fear mongering nature of white on black racism and the rage to set fire to the hated black self by graphically eliminating the other's other of black on black racism. Fanon continues: "A consciousness committed to experience is ignorant, has to be ignorant, of the essences and the determinations of its being." (Fanon 1977 pg. On this134). This consciousness alienated from all that is being other than experience is the most potent gift of the white man to the non-white races which when accepted effectively repeats the process of alienation but with a white supremacist rationale to it thereby rendering both white and non-white ignorant of the reality and potential of their being. The ignorant consciousness driven by self-hate of the non-white is the mechanism of power by which we make ourselves an object of the hegemonic white man. Fanon continues on consciousness: "Still in terms of consciousness, black consciousness is immanent in its own eyes. I am not a potentiality of something. I am wholly what I am. I do not have to look for the universal.

No probability has any place inside of me. My Negro consciousness does not hold itself out as a lack. It *is*. It is its own follower." (Fanon 1977 pg. 135). Negro consciousness is immanent in its own eyes as the white man must refuse that it exists for the incomplete less than the required standard to be human cannot constitute a consciousness in and for themselves. Negro consciousness is complete and capable of defining the Negro as there is no lack in its composition and in the Negro it defines. The reality of Negro consciousness exists, It Is, indicating that no probability exists in the being of the Negro as the Negro is not the potential of something as the Negro IS. Fanon is then insisting that the path to liberation exists and is real as it flows with Negro consciousness. What does this path entail? Fanon states: "Without a Negro past, without a Negro future, it was impossible for me to live my Negrohood. Not yet white, no longer wholly black, I was damned. Between the white man and me the connection was irrevocably one of transcendence." (Fanon 1977 pg. 138). There must be history of and certainty of a future to this path of liberation but there is the reality of the power relation with the hegemonic white man and its impact on the Negro in search of the path to liberation and on the path to liberation. Neither white nor still completely black, the need for a history of the path and the nature of the future of those on the path is then strategic. To perceive and enter the path demand transcendence of the white man and his hegemonic power relations which is a matching move to the white man's transcendence of the Negro. The Negro on the path to liberation must then learn and perfect transcendence. Fanon then presents instances at the end of the chapter to illustrate why transcendence is the strategic necessity. Fanon states: "A feeling of inferiority? No, a feeling of nonexistence. Sin is Negro as virtue is white. All of those white men in a group, guns in their hands, cannot be wrong, I am guilty. I do not know of what, but I know that I am no good." (Fanon 1977 pg. 139). Fanon continues: "The Negro is a toy in the white man's hands; so, in order to shatter the hellish cycle, he explodes." (Fanon 1977 pg. 140). The power wielded by the white man which moulds a pliant Negro because they made themselves objects of the white man, they surrendered to the onslaught. The resident salient question then is the nature of the path to liberation.

Is there then an essence, a core that survives the onslaught of white hegemonic mechanisms of power that serves as the launching pad for the path for liberation? No! What there exists is the reaction on a personal level to the discrimination experienced and the dehumanisation of our non-white selves but how we react and what we do in response hinges on our socialisation. Socialisation that exposed us to a worldview of resistance, of the demystification of the white man's innate superiority and the humanity of the non-white races presents the foundation to resistance that enables visualisation of the path to liberation. There is no quick fix path to liberation for what is required is an alternate worldview that deconstructs the entire knowledge/power apparatus of white hegemonic power. An alternate knowledge articulated by a deracinated language is absolutely necessary to liberation which is highly problematic in the North Atlantic hence Fanon's emphasis on revolution in the colonies of the North Atlantic. Those of us in the North Atlantic must then focus on creating cultures of resistance and liberation where our worldviews are the bulwarks against the ongoing assault on our mind, bodies, spirits.

My maternal grandmother born to a white woman and a mulatto male insisted to me that there was nothing special with, no innate superiority of the white race and the worst case of existence in the context of our colonial and post-colonial social order was to be poor white. My grandmother therefore exposed me to the idea of questioning the innate exceptionalism of white people which came into play when I was exposed to the racist assault of my white paternal family. I never needed to travel to the North Atlantic to encounter a white racist social order, to experience and wrestle with white racist assaults seeking a means to shore up my person and demand my humanity. Worse yet my position in the hierarchy of colour insisted to me that I must hate the Africans and Indian Trinbagonians utilising white racism and accept that the same said discourse of racism I hate with insists to me that I am inferior to the white race and must be servile and suppliant. I must then erect an inferiority complex that envelops my soul but simultaneously I am allowed a superiority complex in my view of the black races. I am required to be a functionally, adaptable, elastic, schizophrenic. I must then accept the soul my white paternal family created for me and sought my willingness to apply it to myself as a drape, a mask over my body. I must make myself an object. Over my teenage years I learnt that I posed a grave problem to the white racist mechanism of power, as part of my genetic code was white with Chinese, African and First Peoples genes thrown in. I can never be white but I can be "nearly white" thereby posing this grave threat for in 1969-1970 when the majority African population were calling for Black Power I realised that my white family was now willing to move me up the ranks to "nearly white", no longer was I the rejected son of a nigger woman I became the tolerated son of a nigger woman. But when the Black Power movement abated it was back to the order with a vengeance because of my foray close to whiteness. What then occurred to me, and it remains with me to this day, is that in a racist social order with multiple hierarchies of colour operationalised I belong nowhere, I am enigma! The path was then in sight by my personal experience and my journeys through Fanon, Marx, Malik el-Shabazz and Mao Zedong and then Foucault and the journey continues. And most of all the most potent weapon unleashed to seduce me to turn myself into an object was to accept the condition of being "nearly white" which was confirmed by my trips to the North Atlantic where I was told that I was "nearly white" not black as I classified myself. I was then expected to perpetually chase after my elusive whiteness, culminating in marriage to a white woman and procreating to wash away my white father's guilt, and in so doing pay a grave personal price for washing the genetic code of my children where you live in perpetual gratitude to the white woman who chose to marry a mongrel.

It is all in the genes but the genes pose grave threats to hierarchies of colour as they split and combine according to their own dynamic, not those of racists of all hues. Now in my sixty-third year of life my white father repeatedly states to me that I am the spitting image of my paternal great grandfather in Madeira for he is in amazement at the product of his procreation across the racist divide with a less than a white woman, even a nigger woman. Such is the power of his white lineage as it overwhelmed nigger genes in my production in my mother's womb. To understand the power of racist fallacy and its impact on worldview you must understand having described the race origins of my grandmother, that my maternal grandfather was Chinese. This then is the potent challenge faced by persons as myself in a postcolonial context, where you are a castaway in the land of your birth, not by choice, but by the racist social order where every day you experience the potency of black on black racism, the most potent legacy of white colonial domination which has assumed a life of its own in the postcolonial context.

Chapter 7
North Atlantic Psychoanalysis and the Negro

In this chapter Fanon analyses the relevance of North Atlantic psychoanalysis to the study of the black man's view of the world. Fanon insists that black reality is not legible to and in keeping with North Atlantic psychoanalysis carried out on white patients. Fanon presents a number of examples which are not in keeping with the paradigm of North Atlantic psychoanalysis. Fanon states: "A normal Negro child, having grown up within a normal family, will become abnormal on the slightest contact with the white world." (Fanon 1977 pg. 143). Again: "A drama is enacted every day in colonised countries. How is one to explain, for example, that a Negro who has passed his baccalaureate and has gone to the Sorbonne to study to become a teacher of philosophy is already on guard before any conflictual elements have coalesced around him?" (Fanon 1977 pg. 145). The paradigm of North Atlantic psychoanalysis simply cannot explain why with contact with whites a non-white becomes plagued with abnormality as defined by the paradigm of North Atlantic psychoanalysis. Or why the non-white who holds a bachelor's degree and is intent on further education in the colonial metropole has expectations of conflict that will negatively impact his life chances in the colonial metropole.

Collective Catharsis

In his quest for explanation Fanon fingers the socialisation of the Negro in the Antilles with reference to collective catharsis. Fanon states: "If we want to answer correctly, we have to fall back on the idea of *collective catharsis*. In every society, in every collectivity, exists-must exist-a channel, an outlet through which the forces accumulated in the form of aggression can be released." (Fanon 1977 pg. 145). Fanon is positing that the mechanisms of collective catharsis in their quest to release aggression formulate children games, cartoons, comic books etc. to attain their end. Fanon states that in the colonies black children are fed games and books created by whites for white children. That is why in these games and books blacks are demonised. Fanon states: "In the magazines the Wolf, the Devil, the Evil Spirit, the Bad

Man, the Savage are always symbolised by Negroes or Indians; since there is always identification with the victor, the little Negro, quite as easily as the little white boy, becomes an explorer, an adventurer, a missionary 'who faces the danger of being eaten by the wicked Negroes.'" (Fanon 1977 pg. 146). The little Negro in the course of experiencing the comic book, the games and the children's books is exposed to a concerted assault on the humanity of his race which he has to wrestle with towards devising a coping strategy. The white instrument of collective catharsis for whites is not a cathartic event for blacks as it spawns an inferiority complex with its attendant self-hate and aggression expressed inwardly and outwardly. Fanon insists that the basis of this condition is the all-white truth embraced by the Negro child. Fanon insists: "There is identification-that is, the young Negro subjectively adopts a white man's attitude." (Fanon 1977 pg. 147). Fanon continues: "Little by little, one can observe in the young Antillean the formation and crystallisation of an attitude and way of thinking and seeing that are essentially white." (Fanon 1977 pg. 148). The young Negro is then being socialised/problematized via the mechanisms of the collective catharsis which destroy the utility of the concept in analysing black reality under white hegemony. The end result is the whitening of the Antillean Negro. The paradigm of North Atlantic psychoanalysis is not part of the non-white solution but part of the assault of white hegemony on non-white peoples. It is simply a scientific medical discourse of power serving white racist hegemony. Fanon continues on the whitening of the Antillean Negro as follows: "Subjectively, intellectually, the Antillean conducts himself as a white man. But he is a Negro. That he will learn once he goes to Europe; and when he hears Negroes mentioned he will recognise that the word includes himself as well as the Senegalese." (Fanon 1977 pg. 148). In the Antilles the Negro is the majority race and their daily contact with the white minority can be entirely non-existent during their daily life whilst they are progressively whitened by white hegemonic discourse. The power relations of white hegemony with the Negro as a minority fully exposed to the racist social order dominated by a white majority is then alien to the Antillean Negro who has never experienced the European order and with arrival in Europe they are in for a rude awakening. Fanon continues: "As long as he remains among his own people, the little black follows very nearly the same course as the little white. But if he goes to Europe he will have to reappraise his lot." Now, the Antillean family has for all practical purposes no connection with the national-that is, the French or European structure. The Antillean has therefore to choose between his family and European society;" (Fanon 1977 pg. 149). There are then two operational spheres acting upon the Antillean Negro described by Fanon. An operational sphere in the Antilles where the whitening process operates unhindered in a social order where Negroes are the demographic majority and whites the significant minority which is then a race based oligarchy. Contact, interaction and transactions with white people are not vital to the success of the whitening process as it is rooted in culture, worldview utilising the mechanism of discourse through all its expressive instruments. And the racist social order of white dominated European society which polices non-whites within a spatial order and structure where non-whites are allotted to specific spaces reserved for them via a mechanism of internal colonialism. The other is relentlessly assailed and policed to ensure the sustainability of the white racist social order. The racist assault is entirely different in Europe from that of the Antilles as it is responding to the threat living in their midst, challenging for space which results in an assault on the other separate and apart from that in the Antilles. This assault tears apart the bonds developed under white assault in the Antilles, as the Negro in France must tear himself away, separate himself from the Antilles subjectively, emotionally and in the psyche thereby constituting an anomic, alienated Negro hollowed out to be refilled with the whitening of France not the Antilles. In this re-whitening the bond of family will be dissolved as all bonds to indicators of Antillean blackness. Fanon now sums up this trend of thought by emphasising the weight of the myth of blackness that weighs on the black man thereby oppressing him. This myth, and its oppressive weight on black people is always most potent in affect in the North Atlantic where blackness oppresses black people. Fanon then deals with the issue of the unconscious where he insists that the daily oppression that the weight of blackness wields on black people in the North Atlantic simply does not allow black people to deal with the ravages of the oppression at the level of the unconscious. This is so because the racist oppression lives and impacts on a daily basis allowing no time for making it unconscious as it is totally conscious in your face at all times. Fanon states: "Since the racial drama is played out in the open, the black man has no time to 'make it unconscious.' The Negro's inferiority or superiority complex or his feeling of equality is *conscious*. These feelings forever chill him. They make his drama. In him there is none of the affective amnesia characteristic of the typical neurotic." (Fanon 1977 pg. 150). Fanon says that the white man is afforded the luxury of guilt, a luxury denied black people as all we are afforded is the conscious. Fanon states that the neurotic constituted by this daily oppressive drama is not the typical neurotic of the North Atlantic psychoanalytical paradigm as the black neurotic is atypical as there is no affective amnesia which demands an alternate black paradigm of psychoanalysis. Forever trapped in the conscious the weight of the oppression of blackness denies us the escape of affective amnesia or the journey of the unconscious to fabricate guilt.

White Psychoanalysis and Negro Reality

Fanon has now arrived at the position that white psychoanalysis cannot plumb the depths of Negro reality much less explain and treat its symptoms. Fanon states: "Whenever I read a psychoanalytic work, discussed problems with my professors, or talked with European patients, I have been struck by the disparity between the corresponding schemas and the reality that the Negro presents. It has led me progressively to the conclusion that there is a dialectical substitution when goes from the psychology of the white man to that of the black." (Fanon 1977 pgs. 150-151). White psychoanalysis cannot grasp the specificity of the Negro reality because white and black are locked into a dialectical relationship hence locked in a contradiction that must be resolved. White reality is not indicative nor expressive of Negro reality as there is no continuum between them, for all there is a power relation premised on a discourse of white racist hegemony exercised over an inferior, epidermalised race. The impact of this discourse on the targeted race must constitute an individual distinct, separate and different from the white race. White racist psychoanalysis applied to black people is simply an attempt to normalise them via various instruments of social control including the asylum.

The Negro and Psychopathology

At this juncture Fanon states his base premise of his paradigm of the Negro and psychopathology as follows: "we can say that every neurosis, every abnormal manifestation, every affective erethism in an Antillean is the product of his cultural situation. In other words, there is a constellation of postulates, a series of propositions that slowly and subtly-with the help of books, newspapers, schools and their texts, advertisements, films, radio-work their way into one's mind and shape's one's view of the world of the group to which one belongs. In the Antilles that view of the world is white because no black voice exists." (Fanon 1977 pgs. 152-153). The realm of culture is the terrain of assault on the Antillean Negro with a structure constituted to assault the mind of the Antillean Negro, to view the world in a specific manner, to adopt a white worldview. This cultural apparatus of assault, this terrain of engagement is then the instrument of white power that assaults, seduces the Antillean Negro to embrace the white worldview. This then is a classic power relation in search of sustainable hegemony by one race over another, simply a continuation by other means of colonial, imperial white domination. The terrain of assault liberates the white race from the need for colonial occupation, thereby enabling the fullest development of assault and seduction through cultural instruments of power which aid and embellish geopolitical domination and economic exploitation. This is simply why in the post-world war 2 era, decolonisation was applied in the epoch of the rise of globalised North Atlantic post-modern power and culture under the hegemony of US exceptionalism. Fanon is insisting that this cultural mechanism of assault and seduction is the rational product of strategic intent. Constituted by power to attain a strategic end: the servility of inferior races necessary to sustainable white hegemony informed by a body of knowledge of the Antillean Negro and any other inferior race targeted for knowledge and power beget each other and are joined: knowledge/ power. The basis of the paradigm of this cultural assault is this discourse of power/knowledge that constitutes the white worldview for the Antillean Negro and all other targeted races. Liberation is then premised on first deconstructing this discourse of power/knowledge where the paradigm of their agenda will be revealed and then methodically assaulting this discourse of power/knowledge to refute it with our alternate discourse of power/ knowledge. The war must be waged at the level of the idea where discordant discourses must interrogate, assault and seduce each other until we disarm the hegemonic discourse of the white cultural apparatus.

The second premise of his paradigm follows the first as it deals with the impact of the European social order on the Antillean Negro migrant. Fanon states: "When the Negro makes contact with the white world, a certain sensitising action takes place. If his psychic structure is weak, one observes a collapse of the ego. The black man stops behaving as an *actional* person. The goal of his behaviour will be The Other (in the guise of the white man), for The Other alone can give him worth. That is on the ethical level: self-esteem." (Fanon 1977 pg. 154). The impact of contact with the white social order as described by Fanon amounts to social control where white supremacist hegemonic discourse assaults the psychic structure in the quest for docile, servile bodies where you are no longer an actional person devoid of the self-esteem necessary to drive action. Fanon uses the concept of the other where in conventional use the Antillean Negro will then be othered quite differently where the white man is The Other who gives definition and purpose to the Antillean Negro. The Other will then define and hold captive his other who feeds off The Other in his quest for self-esteem, for the actional person, for purpose, for definition, for worldview. But the white man is simultaneously othered by hegemonic power which explains Fanon's repetitive reference to the white man as The Other during the text of this work. By constructing this concept Fanon is illustrating the depth and intensity of the assault on the Negro in white society to exercise racist hegemonic social control and the grave task that liberation demands.

Negro Phobogenesis

Fanon states that the issue of the psychoanalysis of the Negro in the works of Freud, Adler and Jung doesn't exist. The current concern with this aspect of psychoanalysis Fanon expressed his distrust of the manner of its application. This distrust of Fanon with the manner of application of psychoanalysis to the Negro drives his task to create a paradigm of the Negro and psychopathology. One such concept in Fanon's paradigm is Negro Phobogenesis where the Negro is a phobogenic object or a stimulus to anxiety in white people or fear of a particular trait of the white stereotype of the Negro. In the text Fanon presents Negro phobogenesis as the third premise of his paradigm of the Negro and Psychopathology. Why do white people articulate phobias over black people? Is it linked to trauma experienced by these white phobics at the hands of black people? Fanon states: "As we can see, the phobic is a person who is governed by the laws of rational prelogic and affective prelogic: methods of thinking and feeling that go back to the age at which he experienced the event that impaired his security." (Fanon 1977 pg. 155). But what explains the reality where white women and men exercise phobias over contact with Negroes on the basis of the threat and fear inferred in the absence of a traumatic event/s in their lives involving a black person? Fanon insists that the choice of the phobic object is overdetermined which means that the white supremacist hegemonic discourse will overdetermine the choice of the Negro, specifically the fear of the Negro, the threat posed by the Negro to the white person as defined by the discourse of the Negro. Fanon in the text focuses on the sexualisation of the Negro by The Other. Fanon states: "That is because the Negrophobic woman is in fact nothing but a putative sexual partner-just as the Negrophobic man is a repressed homosexual. In relation to the Negro, everything takes place on the genital level." (Fanon 1977 pgs. 156-157). The Negro under the hegemonic discourse of white supremacy has been genitalized and sexualised as the discourse insists. Fanon deconstructs the discourse as follows: "As for the Negroes, they have tremendous sexual powers. They are really genital. Be careful, or they will flood us with little mulattoes. Our women are at the mercy of the Negroes." (Fanon 1977 pg. 157). Once they go black they never come back! The threat of the Negro to the white race is framed in terms of sexual prowess and the threat posed to the genetic purity of the white race by the targeting of the white woman by the Negro and the propensity of the white woman to embrace the sexualised/genitalized Negro. This is an assault on the Negro male and white woman, especially those who have Negro partners, have sexual relations with Negroes and mulatto children. This strain of the discourse polices sexual relations by problematizing the Negro through the discursive concept of the sexualised and genitalized Negro which drives Negrophobia, especially in white women, for the discourse also polices her sexuality, sexual choices, the product of her womb and the threat it poses to her race. Fanon states: "For the sexual potency of the Negro is hallucinating. That is indeed the word. The potency must be hallucinating. Sexual anxiety is predominant here." (Fanon 1977 pgs. 157-158). The white is conjuring the sexual potency of the Negro into reality by hallucinating the sexual potency into existence, lived reality and its phobic existence at the personal level. The hegemonic discursive concept drives the hallucination, the phobia and the soul placed on black people which enables social control. One specific concept of hegemonic discourse is the sexualised and genitalized black athlete who is the apex manifestation of the sexualised and genitalized black man. The black athlete triggers desire, hallucinations, phobias and fears with an intensity in keeping with their apex position in the racist hierarchy.

Fanon now deals with the dynamic between the white man and the sexualised and genitalized Negro. Fanon is postulating that the white man is plagued with sexual inferiority and impotence caused by the Negro male which drives white male hate. Fanon states: "Still on the genital level, when a white man hates black men, is he not yielding to a feeling of impotence or of sexual inferiority? Since his ideal is an infinite virility, is there not a phenomenon of diminution in relation to the Negro, who is viewed as a penis symbol? Is the lynching of the Negro not a sexual revenge?" (Fanon 1977 pg. 159). The ideal of infinite male virility drives the collision between the white and black males, as the discourse of the sexualised and genitalized black male impacts negatively the superiority complex of the white male constituting white male complexes of sexual inferiority and impotence. Fanon insists that one way of seeking collective catharsis for this black induced white inferiority complex is simply to castrate the black man in multiple forms summed up in the lynching and the lynch mob. Fanon sums up this premise of his paradigm of the Negro and Psychopathology as follows: "If one wants to understand the racial situation psychoanalytically, not from a universal viewpoint but as it is experienced by individual consciousness, considerable importance must be given to sexual phenomena." (Fanon 1977 pg. 160). The underlying tension, the threat posed by the Negro male and the reaction of the white male to this threat, this fear is then sexually driven as, unlike the Jew, the Negro is never viewed as posing economic, political and intellectual threats. The Negro threat is sexual targeting the white woman and the subsequent production of a Miscegenated race which is the living embodiment and the inability of the white man to sexually dominate the women of his race. The Miscegenated product of copulation across the racial divide between a Negro male and a white woman is the living expression and constant reminder of the white man's sexual shame. A shame that drives race hate and racist violence.

At this point in the text Fanon now defines the constituents of Negrophobia as follows: "let us try to determine what are the constituents of Negrophobia. This phobia is to be found on an instinctual, biological level. At the extreme, I should say that the Negro, because of his body, impedes the closing of the postural schema of the white man-at the point, naturally, at which the black man makes his entry into the phenomenal world of the white man." "What is important to us here is to show that with the Negro the cycle of the *biological* begins." (Fanon 1977 pgs. 160-161). Negrophobia, which afflicts white people arises from the presence of Negroes in the perceptual world of white people, whose presence demands interpretation and action. The discourse of the sexualised and the genitalized Negro, this unique biological specimen with an overdetermined penis, sexual drive and praxis of sexual intercourse (Nature boys) deconstructs the very functionality of, the self-awareness of the white body in spaces where the Negro is encountered. The Negro is then biologicised, who then poses a perceived instinctual and biological threat to white people, some of whom develop phobias to deal with the threat posed and perceived, even though they have never interacted with the Negro. Fear at the instinctual level then drives the process of action formulated to treat with the Negro presence in space shared with a white person. Fanon continues: "But the Negro is castrated. The penis, the symbol of manhood is annihilated, which is to say it is denied." (Fanon 1977 pg. 162). The physical assault arising from this sexual inferiority complex is illustrated by the castration of the Negro, the removal of the penis from the body of the Negro not only destroys manhood, sexual superiority, but constitutes the ideal Negro for white dominated space: penisless in the North Atlantic removes the Negro advantage. Fanon continues on his theme on the threat posed by the sexualised and genitalized Negro as follows: "But it is in his corporeality that the Negro is attacked. It is as a concrete personality that he is lynched. It is as an actual being that he is a threat. The Jewish menace is replaced by the fear of the sexual potency of the Negro." (Fanon 1977 pg. 163-164). The very body, the existence of, the personality of the Negro, their actual being is attacked to be silenced, eliminated in a bid to restore balance to a perceived imbalance afflicting white men. Fanon continues: "The civilised white man retains an irrational longing for unusual eras of sexual license, of orgiastic scenes, of unpunished rapes, of unrepressed incest. Projecting his own desires onto the Negro, the white man behaves 'as if' the Negro really had them." "But the Negro is fixated at the genital; or at any rate he has been fixated there." "The Negro symbolises the biological danger; the Jew, the intellectual danger." (Fanon 1977 pg. 165). The white man therefore transfers his sexual desires that are assaulted by normalising power of the North Atlantic to the Negro insisting that the Negro carries these predilections to sexual license in their very biology, their being and their essence for they are animals. This sexualised soul then heightens the impact and intensity of the normalising assault on Negroes in the white dominated social orders of the North Atlantic. The Negro then begets the need for eugenics and the Final Solution by dint of their biology, their animalism, where their humanity has been reduced to a thing! The phobia of Negroes is then a fear of the specific biological reality and the ensuing threat posed by the Negro. Fanon states: "To suffer from a phobia of Negroes is to be afraid of the biological. For the Negro is only biological. The Negroes are animals." (Fanon 1977 pg. 165).

Fanon at this instance of the text reports that for some three to four years he questioned some five hundred members of the white race of European nationality using the medium of associational tests to determine their position on the Negro. Fanon reports that almost sixty percent of the sample reported as follows: "Negro brought forth biology, penis, strong, athlete, potent, boxer, Joe Louis, Jesse Owen, Senegalese troops, savage, animal, devil, sin. Senegalese soldier, used as the stimulus, evoked dreadful, bloody, tough, strong." (Fanon 1977 pg. 166). Fanon also notes the impact of him being a Negro on the responses of the white test group for when whites administered the test to whites the number of those expressing racist conceptions of the Negro increased. Specific conclusions then arise on what is then a Negro as constituted by the white discourse of the Negro: sexualised and genitalized to the point of being reduced to biology, to being rape, the Negro symbolises the biological. But Fanon insists that articulating these realities is not the prime task at hand as much more is demanded. The strategic task is to deconstruct the mechanics and unearth meanings possessed and utilised by the white discourse of the Negro. Fanon states: "Both authorised and anecdotal literature have created too many stories about Negroes to be suppressed. But putting them all together does not help us in our real task, which is to disclose their mechanics. What matters to us is not to collect facts and behaviour, but to find their meaning." (Fanon 1977 pg. 168). To target the mechanics and meaning of behaviour we must deconstruct the social order linking behaviour to discourse, power /knowledge and power relations. The mechanics of power and power relations and the meanings attached for the individual placed in a social order is impacted by the social order which demands deconstruction. Fanon is insisting that the Negro in a white social order has a specificity attached to the soul of the Negro which drapes the body, which must be recognised towards deconstructing the mechanics and meaning of this black soul, the white man's creation. Fanon states: "But when we assert that European culture has an imago of the Negro which is responsible for all the conflicts that may arise, we do not go beyond reality." (Fanon 1977 pg. 169). European culture then constitutes an image in the unconscious of white people of the sexualised genitalized Negro but what does it constitute in the unconscious of the Negro exposed to this hegemonic hegemony? What is the purpose of this imago of the Negro in the unconscious of white people if not for purposes of social control, for the control of both white people and Negroes to serve the quest of hegemonic power for sustainability? If you deny this link between race, power and social control then you are positing that racism arises from incalculable sources and groundswells. For there must be discourse driven by power/knowledge to insist that there is difference, and that difference is presenting a grave threat, and this power is wielded/exercised in a social order which must be maintained and preserved and you do this with policing ideas, discourse and bodies. The discourse of the Negro owes its existence, longevity and dynamism to its relationship with power: local, national and geopolitical. That is why in the phase of neo-colonialism in the ex-colonies black on black racism is now hegemonic.

The Other

The white man has to erect a defence against this imago, this Negro and so he constructs The Other which, Fanon describes as follows: "The white man is convinced that the Negro is a beast; if it is not the length of the penis, then it is the sexual potency that impresses him. Face to face with this man who is 'different from himself,' he needs to defend himself. In other words, to personify The Other. The Other will become the mainstay of his preoccupation and his desires." (Fanon 1977 pg. 170). The white man must defend against a potent threat devised by white discourse but this defence is also constituted by hegemonic discourse which is The Other. The devised defence has then to police and normalise both the Negro and the white man. The fear of and the threat posed by the Negro impacts and interrogates the white man, where the white man personifies The Other whilst the Negro is the Other's other. Without the impact of the other's other there will be no Other and no preoccupation with the Other's other and the condition of being The Other in itself. Without the discourse of The other and The Other's other to unearth, define, materialise the desires, these desires will have no material reality, hence no impact and traction. The Other and The Other's other will then be placed in an existential realm devoid of such desires which is unthinkable, unimaginable and beyond the extent of experience for the strategy of hegemonic discourse is for both The Other and The Other's other to revel in, to be addicted to and to police themselves by the desires generated by the discourse of the Negro. Simply another instrument of power.

Fanon now describes aspects of Negro existential reality as follows: "I was compelled to *see* that the Antillean is first of all a Negro." "The truth is that the Negro race has been scattered, that it can no longer claim unity." "*Wherever he goes, the Negro remains a Negro.*" (Fanon 1977 pgs. 172-173). The Negro is first and always a Negro regardless of where he lives, what nationality he is and his whiteness for the black soul keeps enveloping his body with white definition and expectations. The Negro is then constituted by white discourse to assault, mute and replace an alternative non-white, African body and worldview deemed a threat. The existential reality of the Negro evokes this statement from Fanon: "An endless task, the cataloguing of reality. We accumulate facts, we discuss them, but with every line that is written, with every statement that is made, one has the feeling of incompleteness." (Fanon 1977 pg. 172). No effort at understanding reality, framed by and located in a social order can ever be complete, finished for all time as power and power relations are ever dynamic, fluid and inconsistent which constitute fluid reality. Illustrated by the fact that the discourse of the Negro is not our creation and out of our control yet it impacts our existential reality.

Unconscious Masochism

Fanon presents this concept whilst considering the case of Negro literature in which the black man fulfils all the Negro stereotypical expectations of white people on white victims. Writing in reference to Br'er Rabbit Fanon states: "In order to protect themselves against their own unconscious masochism, which impels them to rapturous admiration of the (black) rabbit's prowess, the whites have tried to drain these stories of their aggressive potential." (Fanon 1977 pg. 174). Fanon continues: "In the United States, as we can see, the Negro makes stories in which it becomes possible for him to work off his aggression; the white man's unconscious justifies this aggression and gives it worth by turning it on himself, thus reproducing the classical schema of masochism." (Fanon 1977 pg. 176). Fanon is insisting that the white man, The Other, is a masochist which drives his embrace of the aggression towards whites expressed by Br'er Rabbit for it is aimed at white people and satiates his masochistic desire for pain. But every trait exhibited by The Other is reflected in The Other's other and this specific masochism is the product of the discourse of the Negro where masochism in both the white man and the Negro expressed in the power dynamic between both races serves the strategic imperative for social control. The discourse of the Negro constitutes the Negro but it also locks the whites into a dynamic power relation with the constituted Negro that impacts the whites and their dynamic with the social order and ultimately power. The Other and their other are both then the products of hegemonic power and the quest for sustainable social control. Fanon now sums up his position as follows: "We can now stake out a marker. For the majority of white men, the Negro represents the sexual instinct (in its raw state). The Negro is the incarnation of a genital potency beyond all moralities and prohibitions." (Fanon 1977 pg. 177). For the white man the Negro is the expression of a state of being and existence desired, but lost to white supreme, hegemonic civilisation. The Negro is driven by pure sexual instinct and potency and in this desired condition the Negro poses a grave threat to the white race. This grave threat must then be conceptualised via dualities that outstrip this sexual instinct of unrestricted potency where it is combined with the epidermalisation of the Negro to create specific designations of the threat posed by the Negro. Fanon states: "The Negro is the genital. Is this the whole story? Unfortunately, not. The Negro is something else. The black man is the symbol of Evil and Ugliness." (Fanon 1977 pg. 180).

Manicheism Delirium

Fanon continues: "Good-Evil, Beauty-Ugliness, White-Black: such are the characteristic pairings of the phenomenon that, making use of an expression of Dide and Guiraud, we shall call 'manicheism delirium.'" (Fanon 1977 pg.183). The North Atlantic/white people view the world and classify reality in terms of dualities that are mutually irreconcilable yet joined in a dance of existential necessity for one side of the duality cannot exist without the other. This is a worldview that formulates and propagates extremism, suppression, inequality and intolerance as being necessary to the task of expunging the threat posed by the enemy condition of the duality. This worldview of reality as being predicated on dualities that cannot be synthesised, when combined with a linear concept of time where space is subservient to time, and the cosmology of the perfect clockwork driven by universal law constitutes white racist supremacist discourse of the European Enlightenment. This Manicheism drives the white discourse of the Negro, a special and unique formulation of the central and prime duality of this discourse: White/Black. But this manicheism of the white man's discourse of the Negro constitutes delirium in white people in their quest to resolve the White/Black duality in their favour through the only means their manicheism allows as the Negro is lynched. The failure to resolve the White/Black duality in the manner called for by the white worldview also constitutes delirium in the minds of white people. One is the delirium of ecstasy, the other is illusions, restlessness and incoherence. The dual worldview of white people demands that the White/Black duality must be resolved violently in favour of white people in order to ensure the continuity of the Manicheism delirium, for Black lives do not matter in this condition of Manicheism delirium. By branding a race your binary opposite which constitutes your existential enemy, epidermalising that race whilst investing that race with special, unique sexual potential, appetites and a sexual organ which pose a threat to your male hegemony over white women, your discourse of the Negro demands the application of the Final Solution to this grave, existential threat. This discursive necessity that assails white people across time, impacts the white unconscious where the disparity between the discourse of the Negro and that of the discourse of law, sovereignty and human rights must be rationalised at the level of the psyche. The psyches of North Atlantic white people are then battlegrounds of conflicting discursive strategies, outcomes and permitted and acceptable behaviours where they traverse a spectrum ranging from ambivalence to schizophrenia to multiple personalities where their racism demands that they live lies as the foundation of daily life. The flow of Arab and African migrants to Europe in the second decade of the 21st century has now forced their racism out of the neat boxes placed on its expression after the demise of National Socialism as the hegemonic discourse of Europe. The African and the Arab are now presenting grave existential threats and Manicheism delirium is manifesting itself potently in the politics of Europe where there is the ecstasy derived from racist attacks on migrants, the Roma and increasingly on Jews, last seen in the mass rallies of Nazi Germany, Croatia, Ukraine and Hungary. And the restlessness, illusions and incoherence arising from the denial of the lust for the Final Solution for the binary opposites that construct the white man's worldview and orders reality for them, are driven by blood lust where every form of life is subject to the Final Solution on this planet in the quest for hegemony. A hegemony that remains defined by desire even lust constituted by the discourse of white supremacy. White racism is central to their worldview and can only be operationalised to attain its design end with the Final Solution. Simply immerse yourself in Gaza where a race burdened with hallucinatory whiteness has embraced manicheism delirium as the fitting expression of its whiteness and its fitness to apply the Final Solution. Whilst in Europe the message is growing louder that your actions in Gaza is just another case of neo-colonial black on black racism with every attack on a Jew and symbols of Jewish culture and presence, in spite of the white man's vocal repudiation of the Final Solution.

Fanon insists that there is no single type of Negro for there is diversity and there will be no understanding of the reality that impacts the Negro by insisting that anti-Semitism and Negrophobia are the same instruments applied to different targets. For Fanon the specificity of the Negro has to be the focus where it speaks for itself and in this task this book is one such act. Fanon states: "This book, it is hoped, will be a mirror with a progressive infrastructure, in which it will be possible to discern the Negro on the road to disalienation. When there is no longer a 'human minimum' there is no culture." (Fanon 1977 pg. 184). Fanon is creating a mirror by which we view ourselves critically absolved of despair as the progressive infrastructure constructed in the book leads to the path of disalienation for those of us earnestly seeking redemption from hallucinatory whiteness. The core reality is the preservation of the humanity at the heart of the project for without this we cannot build the alternate culture that disalienation realised demands. This is the reason for Fanon rejecting the drive of black intellectuals to universalise themselves whilst denying, hence evading the task of seeking to deconstruct their black specificity. Fanon states: "The Negro is universalising himself," "There is a drama there, and the black intellectuals are running the risk of being trapped by it. What? I have barely opened eyes that had been blindfolded, and somebody already wants to drown me in the universal? What about the others? Those who "have no voice," those who "have no spokesman." "...I need to lose myself in my negritude, to see the fires, the segregations, the segregation, the rapes, the discriminations, the boycotts. We need to put our fingers on every sore that mottles the black uniform. It is my belief that a true culture cannot come to life under present conditions. It will be time enough to talk of the black genius when the man has regained his rightful place." (Fanon 1977 pgs. 186-187). Fanon asks the question of what is the position of black genius in the universal chorus? The pursuit of being universalised is in fact the pursuit of whiteness for the universal being pursued is the product of white hegemonic discourse to which the discourse of the Negro is attached. There can be no liberation via the quest for white universalisation for in this quest Negro specificity is denied and out of this denial the culture necessary for liberation cannot be constructed, much less thrive. The Black quest for universalisation is then a quest for whiteness, hallucinatory whiteness. A quest that ensures white hegemony over black supplicants where the blacks make themselves objects and police themselves in deference to white normalisation. Fanon gives an example of this state or condition of the operational condition of the black afflicted with hallucinatory whiteness as follows: "so a Negro like Rene Maran, who has lived in France and breathed and eaten the myths of racist Europe, and assimilated the collective unconscious of that Europe, will be able, if he stands outside himself, to express only his hatred of the Negro." (Fanon 1977 pg. 188). The product of hallucinatory whiteness is black on black racism driven by self-hate, even self-immolation, a state of assault devised as an instrument of white hegemonic power much more operationally effective than white on black racism and especially strategically important in neo-colonial black dominated political orders of majority black social orders.

Fanon now returns to the issue of the discourse of the Negro that drives manicheism delirium. Fanon states: "*In Europe, the black man is the symbol of Evil.* One must move softly, I know, but it is not easy. The torturer is the black man, Satan is black, one talks of shadows, when one is dirty one is black-whether one is thinking of physical dirtiness or of moral dirtiness." "In Europe, whether concretely or symbolically, the black man stands for the black side of the character. As long as one cannot understand this fact, one is doomed to talk in circles about the 'black problem.'" "The archetype of the lowest values is represented by the Negro." (Fanon 1977 pgs. 188-189). The binary opposites of White/Black generate an existential threat for the white race in all that the Negro race is, projects, poses and symbolises. This grave existential threat presents itself in all its potency when the Negro enters the white dominated spaces of Europe, when in the 21st century the Negro and the Arab are now invading these spaces as a wave, even a tsunami of migrants. This grave existential threat demands hate and racist violence from white people for the preservation of the white homeland. But given the demographic fact that it is a black planet, the invasion of, and multiplication of this black threat to Europe in Europe in the 21st century, demands the application of the Final Solution.

Manicheism in 21st century Europe is now demanding the application of the Final Solution to Africans and Arabs, the end of migration of inferior races, multiculturalism and the end of the 20th century instrument of power of internal colonialism and the Banlieues. The European social order must now be purged of the growing threat at the heart of the social order. White manicheism driven by its paranoid race hate, coupled to white supremacy, can only embrace and posit endemic hate and violence constituting the white problem and its vassal hallucinatory whiteness. Both problems are enmeshed with and generate hate and violence. Fanon continues: "In Europe the Negro has one function: that of symbolising the lower emotions, the baser inclinations, the dark side of the soul. In the collective unconscious of *homo occidentalis*, the Negro-or, if one prefers, the colour black- symbolises evil, sin, wretchedness, death, war, famine." (Fanon 1977 pgs. 190-191). The colour black in the white man's worldview represents the threat but why then epidermalise the Negro where all that is signalled by black is attached to the skin of the Negro and they become the living embodiment of all that black is to the white man? A black soul envelops the Negro and they become black posing this grave existential threat that demands race hate, white supremacy and the Final Solution. Why? The strategic end is obvious for in the grip of fear of a black planet you devise a discourse with its mechanism of power to assault the majority black races enabling the hegemony of the white race. The issue is then the exercise of power and the accrual of the benefits of hegemonic power: world domination. The next question is how is the Negro epidermalised?

Collective Unconscious

Fanon answers this question by focusing on the collective unconscious. Fanon defines the collective unconscious as follows: "The collective unconscious is not dependent on cerebral hereditary; it is the result of what I shall call the unreflected imposition of a culture." (Fanon 1977 pg. 191). There is then a specific culture that is imposed without reflection, questioning and opposition that forms the collective unconscious. This culture and its worldview is defined by, and driven by, a discourse of power that defines and frames the collective unconscious for a specific strategic end. This strategic end Fanon describes as follows: "Hence there is no reason to be surprised when an Antillean exposed to walking-dream therapy relives the same fantasies as a European. It is because the Antillean partakes of the same collective unconscious as the European." "All birds of prey are black in Martinique, whose collective unconscious makes it a European country," (Fanon 1977 pg. 191). The collective unconscious of Martinique is European even though it is an island in the Eastern Caribbean whose population is predominantly black, but it is an overseas department of France presently, whilst being a Caribbean colony of France in the past. The colonial domination of Martinique by France, established the hegemony of the European collective unconscious, and the hegemonic collective unconscious of Europe in Martinique ensured the sustainable domination of Martinique by France to the 21st century. This sustainable domination of Martinique by France, ensured by the hegemonic European collective unconscious, was achieved through the socialisation of non-white Martiniquans to make themselves objects of French domination. This is illustrated by the example Fanon provides of the Antillean who relives the same fantasies as Europeans which indicates that the same collective unconscious in Europe is operational in the Antilles, specifically in Martinique, constituting humans even though they are black having the same worldview, discourse and objective reality as Europeans in Europe, even though they are in Martinique. Alienated from their black selves and the nature of the space they are inhabiting. They are then spatially, perceptually and self-hood alienated which constitutes the condition of being an object of white power, of being servile and subservient. Fanon continues: "It is normal for the Antillean to be anti-Negro. Through the collective unconscious the Antillean has taken over all the archetypes belonging to the European. The *anima* of the Antillean Negro is almost always a white woman. In the same way, the *animus* of the Antilleans is always a white man. But I too am guilty, here I am talking of Apollo! There is no help for it. I am a white man. For unconsciously I distrust what is black in me, that is, the whole of my being. I am a Negro-but of course I do not know it, simply because I am one." (Fanon 1977 pg. 191). The Antillean Negro is anti-Negro thereby rejecting self, being and all that constitutes black by white hegemonic discourse. This is the product of the hegemony of white discourse but the collective consciousness applied and hegemonic in the Antilles is operationally different from that in Europe. In the Antilles the white collective unconscious is operationally mobilised over a black dominated population applying white archetypes to the black majority population. The collective consciousness is assaulting the black majority population with its discourse of the Negro towards a specific strategic end. Fanon states that the anima or the feminine side of an Antillean Negro male is almost always a white woman. The animus or the feminine side of the Antillean black woman is almost always a white man. At the core of the unconscious of the Antillean Negro woman and male is the white archetype driven by the discourse of the Negro relentlessly assaulting their psyches, driving the spectrum of maladies that plague us as non-whites in a world under white racist hegemony. Fanon insists that he is a prime example of this condition where he does not know he is a Negro simply because he is one therefore his race does not impact his consciousness of self as there is a defining white that separates both power. He distrusts all that is black in him therefore he must relentlessly drive to purge his blackness and immerse his epidermalised self in whiteness. Fanon insists that he is white! There is no self-consciousness and self- determination for all of us non-whites for we are perennially battling against the battering of our psyches to rid ourselves of the emasculated self, the object that we made ourselves into and the monster we police ourselves to be to ensure its sustainability in the service of white racist hegemony. We are then seriously flawed, damaged goods in need of liberation.

Blacks: The Scapegoat of the Whites

Fanon describes the power relation between white and black and the response of the black man as follows: "Without turning to the idea of the collective catharsis, it would be easy to show that, without thinking, the Negro selects himself as an object capable of carrying the burden of original sin. The white man chooses the black man for this function, and the black man who is white also chooses the black man. The black Antillean is the slave of this cultural imposition. After having being the slave of the white man, he enslaves himself. The Negro is in every sense of the word a victim of white civilisation." (Fanon 1977 pg. 192). The Negro chooses himself and makes himself an object of white racist normalisation, the living epidermalised expression of original sin as defined by the discourse of the Negro. The white man chooses the black man for this task, whilst black men, including whitened black men, choose themselves for the task such is the potent nature of the power relation. The black Antillean makes himself a slave to the imposed white racist culture without questioning, thereby willingly constituting himself a victim of white racist civilisation. What then is this original sin that blacks choose to bear? Fanon states: "the Antillean has recognised himself as a Negro, but, by virtue of an ethical transit, he also feels (collective unconscious) that one is a Negro to the degree to which one is wicked, sloppy, malicious, instinctual. Everything that is the opposite of these Negro modes of behaviour is white. This must be recognised as the source of Negrophobia in the Antilles. In the collective unconscious, black=ugliness, sin, darkness, immorality. In other words, he is

Negro who is immoral. If I order my life like that of a moral man, I simply am not a Negro." (Fanon 1977 pg. 192). The Negro is sin, the original sin of the discourse of the Negro, the living expression of all that is not worthy of being white therefore affirming the inherent superiority of white folks. Being the expression and repository of all evil his skin expresses the sin, the evil which the Negro must bear for the benefit of the white race, for the Negro is the literal scapegoat of the white race enabling their undying adherence to their inherent racial superiority, the master race of a black planet bathed in the impunity of manifest destiny that no non-white race can claim for themselves within the embrace of white racist hegemony. Whilst the non-white races remain encumbered, judged by and the recipients of white imperialism based on our moral failings as judged by hegemonic white discourse. The ethical transit is then the instrument of power that ensures that the definition of the Negro arising from white hegemonic discourse ensures that the realisation of being Negro is an opportunity to assault the individual to accept the hegemonic discourse of the Negro as sin, evil, ugliness and all that is immoral, thereby constituting the Negro as the scapegoat of the white race. This process of power Fanon defines as ethical transit where via the collective unconscious the Negro becomes sin, evil and ugliness, the great rejected one.

Fanon describes the process of the Negro as the scapegoat of the Whites as follows: "More directly, each individual has to charge the blame for his baser drives, his impulses, to the account of an evil genius, which is that of the culture to which he belongs (we have seen that this is the Negro). This collective guilt is borne by what is conventionally called the scapegoat. Now the scapegoat for white society-which is based on myths of progress, civilisation, liberalism, education, enlightenment, refinement-will be precisely be the forces that opposes the expansion and the triumph of these myths. The brutal opposing force is supplied by the Negro." (Fanon 1977 pg. 194). The discourse of the white race for itself constitutes a unique scapegoat as its discourse of the white race is founded upon binary dualities which are expressed as being rooted in a binary race duality: white/black. The scapegoat necessary to the discourse of the white race, the psychology of the white race and the white social order demands that the scapegoat and the Satan/evil genius that made white people respond to and be captive of their base desires is the Negro. The Negro then is the opposing force, the stumbling block to the white man's quest to realise the inherently superior qualities that is the preserve of his race. For the white race is THE personification and locomotive of progress, modernity and civilisation in the world, the gift to the world which endows this race with the right and impunity of manifest destiny. The Negro as scapegoat and personification of evil demands the epidermalisation of the Negro as the epidermalised Negro evolves the operations of the scapegoat and personification of evil via the black skin to discursive developments which ensured that the white psyche and the social order evolve instruments of power that constantly evolved racism as an instrument of power. Racism then became cultural, an essential construct of culture which ensured that it evolved with culture, never hardening, always dynamic. This construct of Fanon further exposes that the white man is not constituted by racism, therefore if you deal with the racism there is a salvageable core that emerges. The white man is constituted by a discourse that utilises racism as an instrument of power, for the discursive concept at the core of the discourse insists that the white man is essentially problematic as death is paramount in its power over all white people as all non-white people. The quest to mask the reality of the finality of death, which trumps all in their quest for immortality, leads to various subservient discursive concepts formulated to deal with this unrelenting finality of all humans. The continued finality of death of white people then drives the construction of the racist construct of the world and its deployment as an instrument of power. But this construct and instrument of power remains driven by the finality of death and the failure of the white man to defeat his death. The solution is not then to cure the white man of his racist discourse, worldview and the instrument of power, for the power of death remains driving the white man's fixation with the finality of his death. As long as death remains all powerful over the white man, his discourse and its racist structure will be the understood, the given, hence hegemonic constituting the white man and his worldview. To liberate the white man from his white supremacist discourse demands liberating her/him from the finality of death, the power of death. Such is the rabbit hole the white race has constructed for itself and seduces us all to condemn ourselves to in their binary polarity.

The Mechanism of Individuation

Fanon now continues with the description of the objecthood of the Negro. Fanon states: "Cultural imposition is easily accomplished in Martinique. The ethical transit encounters no obstacles. But the real white man is waiting for me. As soon as possible he will tell me that it is not enough to try to be white, but that a white totality must be achieved. It is only then that I shall recognise the betrayal. -Let us conclude. An Antillean is made white by the collective unconscious, by a large part of his individual consciousness, and by the virtual totality of his mechanism of individuation. The colour of his skin, of which there is no mention in Jung, is black. All the inabilities to understand are born of this blunder." (Fanon 1977 pg. 193). The reward awaiting all Negroes who accept the white man's discourse of the Negro is soon made manifest. Having made themselves objects/subjects of white power, Negroes soon learn that their surrender bears no benefit and no reward to the Negro, for their servility to the white man makes it clear to the servile Negro that they are obstacles and stumbling blocks to the ultimate quest for a white totality. A white social order in which whiteness has no need to tolerate and deescalate the threat of the of infection posed by the Negro. The quest for the white totality faced with the infection of non-white races must then embrace the Final Solution. All the effort to be white is then useless and of no avail to the white man for our skin has not changed its colour in response to our perceptual, discursive and psychological whiteness and our skin is our sin. The real white man wants his white totality and cannot be satisfied with the product of the collective unconscious working in concert with ethical transfer, the Negro. This is a device of application to the Antilles and all other parts of the globe under colonial and neo colonial domination as the white heartland must remain the ancestral white totality. This then is the fundamental problem posed in the USA as the ancestral white totality remains a mythic discourse whose reality exists in racist delusion. This quest for the ancestral white totality in the USA has then to relentlessly pursue a variety of strategic paths to immunise the white heartland from the infection of non-white races vitally necessary to attain the ancestral white totality. Faced with the demographic time bomb of being soon rendered

a minority race in America in the 21st century the white race is now flirting with the Final Solution. Fanon states that the collective unconscious acting in concert with the individual consciousness of the Negro and the mechanism of individuation which is a virtual totality with all three acting in concert must be operationally understood in the context of the individual being constituted a Negro. All three are then specific to a Negro, the products of white power operationally pursuing a strategic end. The collective unconscious through cultural imposition places the Negro under assault to ensure the whitening of the Negro, the problematizing of the Negro, blackness and the black self and to convince the Negro to make himself an object. The individual consciousness of the Negro subservient to white knowledge/power accepts the strategic need to make himself an object/subject of white power because of the expected benefits to self. And finally the process of individuation, where the individual is distinct and separated from the crowd, which is a process of power especially potent in the North Atlantic, where the individual with self, drives, desire, self-interest, self-love and ultimately narcissism is the strategic end sought. But the Negro individuation has its own unique specificity because this process involves individuation of an epidermalised individual whose skin potently voids the white individuation mechanism. This then is individuation to constitute a flawed, subservient, servile individual, the subject of white power and in the event the process fails there is always the Final Solution on an individual basis. The mechanism of individuation can only constitute a damaged individual as the Negro is problematized to the point of being non-human and inhuman, the Negro has been thingified. This is then the reason why the mechanism of individuation for the Negro can only be a virtual totality, for our inhumanity constitutes us Frankenstein monsters before and hence at the end of the process. The totality for and of non-whites exists only in our delusions with a white gloss and taint ensuring that it is a virtual totality that we trap ourselves in which relentlessly seduces us to live in the nightmare we constitute and insist is La La Land. In this reality of the Negro white psychiatric discourse is irrelevant as an explanatory tool for at the heart of this medicalising discourse is the blunder of failing to see the specificity of the Negro under the hegemony of white racist discourse.

Alienation and Ethical Transfer

Fanon describes the impact of ethical transfer on the Negro as follows: "Moral consciousness implies a kind of scission, a fracture of consciousness into a bright part and an opposing black part. In order to achieve morality, it is essential that the black, the dark, the Negro vanish from consciousness. Hence a Negro is forever in combat with his own image." (Fanon 1977 pg. 194). The Negro has a consciousness that is part white which is in opposition to the black part constituting a Negro with a consciousness at war with itself and with his black self. To defeat the inherently evil, ugly black part of his consciousness the Negro has to deny his black self, his black skin and escape into whiteness which offers no salvation, no respite. To become a moral being, the Negro has to do battle with his black self, his black skin which is an impossible task condemning the Negro to alienation driven by self-hate, futility, hopelessness, withdrawal and self-destruction. Fanon describes this image that the Negro does battle with as follows: "It is just that over a series of long days and long nights the image of the biological-sexual-sensual-genital-nigger has imposed itself on you and you do not know how to get free of it." (Fanon 1977 pg. 202). The image imposed on the Negro, this cultural imposition insists that the Negro is devoid of intellectual capacity and creativity, reducing the Negro to biology but especially a specific aspect of biology the sexual, the sensual, the genital which sums up the nigger. The Negro is then the prime target for death as they lack the intellectual capacity to relentlessly strive to break the finality of death. The nigger is then the prime, perfect expression of Death's victim which the white man must not and cannot be. The white man is then the binary duality with the Negro being all that the Negro is not and cannot ever be. The white man is then the living expression of the capacity to finally break the finality of death on humanity and must never surrender this grave historic task. This task justifies all the instruments of power deployed to ensure hegemony of the white race. The issue is not then to cure racism as it's simply an instrument of power and is incurable. The issue is - can the white man accept and abide by his mortality, the finality and hegemony of death?

Negro Problem

Fanon will then sum up the reality of the binary duality of races white/black as follows: "The Negro problem does not resolve itself into the problem of Negroes living among white men but rather of Negroes exploited, enslaved, despised by a colonialist, capitalist society that is only accidentally white."

94

(Fanon 1977 pg. 202). The problem is not then generated by Negroes living amongst white people the Negro problem is the power relations that exploit, enslave and hate Negroes of a colonial capitalist social order. The issue is not then racism and hate, but of the power relations of a social order that utilises racism and hate as an instrument of power necessary to the enslavement and exploitation of the Negro in a capitalist order. Race hate and capitalism is not a binary duality but a functional wholeness, a totality locked in a power relation towards the exploitation of labour, the maximisation of profits and the generation of wealth on a sustainable basis in keeping with the structure of the social order. The sustainable generation of wealth is impossible without a sustainable social order which is structured and populated by docile individuals. The social order is then the product of power relations and all that the Negro is in this social order is the product of power relations and must have a strategic end, a purpose that serves power. There is then no racism for racism sake. Racism, the Negro must then serve power for it to wield specificity to be a subject of power in the social order. To understand the social order, it is then instructive to unravel the North Atlantic modern and post-modern capitalist order for there is a specific discourse that structures this order, its reality and truth. The point of control is not then the imposition of a culture or the decision to make oneself an object, but the point at which we accept the white man's binary duality of death/life and its life fetishism and act upon it. The point at which we worship life regardless of our quality of life is the point at which are an object/subject of the white man's hegemonic power for we are willing to accept the harshest daily living conditions across generations wallowing in self-hate and hand wringing forever eschewing resistance. Enmeshed in the white man's life fetishism we are willing to accept genocide in the quest for life at all costs. The end result of this condition is described by Fanon as follows: "It proves that, at its extreme, the myth of the Negro, the idea of the Negro, can become the decisive factor of an authentic alienation." (Fanon 1977 pg. 204). The discourse of the Negro is then the basis of the alienation of the Negro which is the basis of the objecthood of the Negro and the quest for hallucinatory whiteness. But alienation from what? Alienation from all that distinguishes the African from the Negro, for the Negro is the product constituted by white hegemonic discourse. The Negro is the product of alienation, the subject of white power and the object of the white man.

Fanon ends the chapter with a statement that illustrates the potency of the objecthood of the Negro as follows: "What is all this talk of a black people, and of a Negro nationality? I am a Frenchman. I am interested in French culture, French civilisation, the French people. We refuse to be considered 'outsiders,' we have full part in the French drama." "I am personally interested in the future of France, in French values, in the French nation. What have I to do with a black empire?" (Fanon 1977 pg. 203). I am not a race, I am a nationality, I am French and I belong to France. If I am a race, my race prevents me from being French as I am at the door to the nation exerting all my efforts to be white to win entrance and to be deemed white, fit to inhabit the white space. I must then constantly shout my white credentials in my bid to win acceptance as I am committed to French civilisation, culture and people, for I desire to be French for that is all I am. I have no other choice for I am the product of French domination. I refuse to accept the reality of white exclusion premised on my epidermalisation and the fact that I can never evade the exclusion the white totality demands, hence my epidermalisation. I pursue whiteness driven by my desire for life at whatever cost, even though this condition of black skin white masks cannot reward me with the condition of life that I desire and lust after. To bear this life conundrum on a daily basis I then devise alternate realities with multiple instruments of escape from this pressing reality. I then become a hollowed out human, a zombie mired in self-immolation, hand wringing and impotence for there is no escape from this condition for I reject the outlet death brings and revolution is inconceivable!

Chapter 8
Interrogating A. Adler and G. W. F. Hegel

In the penultimate chapter of the text being analysed Fanon interrogates the works of Adler and Hegel to determine the relevance of these works to his project of liberation of the Negro. What is especially relevant in this chapter is Fanon's position on Hegel, given Hegel's position as a discursive agent of the discourse of white supremacy with its ancillary discourse of the Negro, especially expressed in his work: "Philosophy of Subjective Spirit." Fanon first delves into Adlerian psychology and I will so follow the path adopted in Fanon's text.

Adlerian Psychology and the Negro

Fanon first states the Adlerian worldview, paradigm and its attendant methodology as follows: "The whole picture of the neurosis, as well as all its symptoms, emerges as under the influence of some final goal, the quality of a principle of orientation, of arrangement, of coordination." "If, on the one hand, one accepts the hypothesis of a final goal or of a causal finality, one sees the shadows dissolve at once and we can read the soul of the patient as the pages of a book." (Fanon 1977 pg. 210). Adler is seeking order driven by universal laws in the psyche of the patient, for that is the only ontology and epistemology that allows causal explanation and the drive for causality which manufactures causal explanations where none clearly presents itself. The final causality is formulated by the external expert gazing upon the patient externally of, and alienated from the psyche under the gaze. Where the medicalising discourse invents science to justify its discourse of power and its role as an instrument of power. Hence the principles of orientation, arrangement and coordination, which constitute the final causality, which is the soul draped over the body/psyche of the patient.

The Adlerian Line of Orientation

Fanon then presents the Adlerian discourse of the Negro as follows: "The Negro is comparison. There is the first truth. He is comparison: that is: he is constantly preoccupied with self-evaluation and with the ego-ideal. The

Antilleans have no inherent values of their own, they are always contingent on the presence of The Other. Every position of one's own, every effort at security is based on relations of dependence, with the diminution of the other. It is the wreckage of what surrounds me that provides the foundation of my virility." (Fanon 1977 pg. 211). The Negro is constantly driven by the need to compare herself/himself to others he interacts with, the compulsive need for constant self-evaluation and ego validation whenever he interacts with others. The drive for incessant comparison is linked to the fact that the values of the Antillean are those garnered from The Other, in the absence of The Other the Antillean Negro is void of values, hence for the Antillean Negro to be there must be The Other. The Negro is then constituted by relations of dependence, the very security of the Negro is rooted in relations of dependence and the diminution of the Negro as the other, the vassal and utter dependent of The Other. All that is the Negro, all that constitutes the Negro is then in shambles, the wreckage that engulfs the other. Fanon presents the second characteristic of the Antillean Negro as follows: "The Antillean is characterised by the desire to dominate the other. His line of orientation runs through the other. It is always a question of the subject; one never even thinks of the object. The object is denied in terms of individuality and liberty. The object is an instrument. It should enable me to realise my subjective security. I am the Hero. I am the centre of attention. I am Narcissus, and what I want to see in the eyes of others is a reflection that pleases me." (Fanon 1977 pg. 212). The object is the captive of the subject, as the subject is seeking accolades and affirmation of her/his innate superiority and in this quest for affirmation and confirmation the object must be abased which confirms the inherent superiority of the subject and grants security of the subject for the subject abhors competition. This is not then an "other" but a backboard and a sounding board that echoes the call of inherent superiority of the subject. Fanon continues: "Therefore, in any given group (environment) in Martinique, one finds the man on top, the court that surrounds him, the in-betweens (who are waiting for something better), and the losers. These last are slaughtered without mercy. Me, nothing but me." (Fanon 1977 pg. 212). Fanon describes the hegemonic human operational environment of Martinique which illustrates that the power relations of the slave plantation continue to exert hegemony over the human operational environment. The structure of the dominant male at the centre of the power relations commanding concentric rings of humans, as the primary ring of his most trusted objects, then the ring of in-betweeners who are differentiated from the bottom feeders/the losers and the primary ring and finally the losers. On the slave plantation there were hierarchies within the primary ring as the most trusted were those of the enslaved who lived in the great house with massa and tended to his needs. Whilst there were those who were equally trusted living on the plantation possessing strategic skills and knowledge vital to the profitability of the plantation. The in-betweeners comprised the children and family of the primary ring and persons noted for strategic skills but under probation until the necessary trust of massa was established for upward mobility, former members of the primary ring who are now aged or physically handicapped placed in retirement by massa to show her/his gratitude for services rendered, thereby illustrating the inherent humanity and superiority of the white race, and finally those who do not distinguish themselves from the mass with special skills of strategic importance but they are docile, avoid all acts of rebellion against the hegemony of massa, and carry out the tasks allocated to them even though massa demands better from them. The losers are drawn from the primary ring, the in-betweeners and those who never attained the approval of massa because they simply never sought it. The hard core losers are those who are in perpetual revolt against the hegemony of massa and their enslavement presenting a grave quandary to massa given the fact that the cost of an enslaved African was a burdensome capital investment for massa. Massa and white society lived in grave fear of the losers as the losers held on to their African culture as the matrix of their rebellion. The other two were those who became losers after expecting too much from massa and then realising that with massa there is no gratitude and legitimate expectation where they then go into rebellion mode and fall downwards into the group of losers. It must be noted that losers in rebellion would commit public graphic suicides on the planation at strategic times as during the sugar cane crop season in full view of the inmates of the planation thereby extinguishing the power of massa of life and death over the African. The post enslavement Martinican social order has retained and modified the power relations of the slave plantation, but the power centre is a Martinican Negro in the leading role of massa whilst being massa's other. Whilst the losers continue to be dominated by those who refuse to, or simply cannot play the game that was first formulated under massa and his slave plantation. Fanon continues as follows: "The Martinicans are greedy for security. They want to compel the acceptance of their fiction. They want to be recognised in their quest for manhood. Each one of them wants to *be*, to *emerge*. Everything that an Antillean does is done for The Other. Not because The Other is the ultimate objective of his action in the sense of communication between people that Adler describes, but, more primitively, because it is The Other who corroborates him in his search for self-validation." (Fanon 1977 pgs. 212-213). Adler's description of the communication interaction between people simply cannot describe this Martinican power relation as those engaged in the power relation, possibly except a number of the losers, are all captive of a common quest for security, for recognition in order to be, to emerge. From what? The Martinican is servile to The Other for everything she/he does is for The Other as an interpretation of what The Other wants and expects, a legitimate expectation of reward drives the perceptions and actions of the Martinican. The Other has and wields the power of corroboration over all the actions of the Martinican thereby establishing the legitimate expectation of self-validation which remains an expectation for validation is a process external of self not intrinsic to self, which means there is no self-determination. This ensures that the power relations of the Martinicans are then noted for their aggression, self-hate, self-immolation, narcissism and the potency of the discourse of black on black racism that drives these power relations. In keeping with Adler's paradigm Fanon states: "Now that we have marked out the Adlerian line of orientation of the Antillean, our task is to look for its source." (Fanon 1977 pg. 213). Fanon has presented the line of orientation of the Antillean in keeping with Adler's paradigm which is already showing signs of questionable applicability to the reality of the Antillean Negro in the context of the social order and its historical legacy. Raising the question of creating a line of orientation in keeping with Adler's paradigm without placing the individual in the power relations of the social order and its historical legacy that impacts the structure of the social order. Fanon in the text next delves into finding the source of the orientation.

The Adlerian Source

In presenting the source Fanon states: "Here the difficulties begin. In effect, Adler has created a psychology of the individual. We have just seen that the feeling of inferiority is an Antillean characteristic. It is not just this or that Antillean who embodies the neurotic formation, but all Antilleans. Antillean society is a neurotic society, a society of 'comparison.' Hence we are driven from the individual back to the social structure. If there is a taint, it lies not in the 'soul' of the individual but rather in that of the environment." (Fanon 1977 pg. 213). Fanon now points out the fundamental falsehood perpetuated by Adler's psychology of the individual applied to the Antillean. It cites the source as the neurotic formation in the individual, but Fanon insists that the society is neurotic, not simply a number of individuals in the social order, and to find the source of a neurotic social order you have to walk away from Adler's psychology of the individual for the source is the social structure of the social order and its historical legacy. Focusing on the neurotic individual generates falsehoods of source, orientation and ultimately the efficacy of treatment prescribed. You have to deal with the mechanism that generates the neurotic environment, hence power and the strategy of the neurotic Antillean. Fanon continues his critique: "All the facts that I have noted are real, but, it should not be necessary to point out, they have only a superficial connection with Adlerian psychology. The Martinican does not compare himself with the white man *qua* father, leader, God; he compares himself with his fellow against the pattern of the white man." (Fanon 1977 pg. 215). The basis of the neuroses of the Antillean does not fit Adler's paradigm of being neurotic for in the Antilles the Negro does not compare himself with the white man in terms set by and defined by Adler as father, leader and God. The Antillean Negro compares himself with other Antilleans by measuring himself and the others against a pattern of the white man, a discourse of what constitutes the white man as superior and hegemonic. To find the source in keeping with Adler's paradigm you then need to depart from Adler's paradigm to deconstruct this pattern, this discourse of the white man into its constituent discursive constructs, trace their historical legacy and finally assess their impact on the psyche of the Antillean within the power relations of the social order as the discourse is rooted in the social order. Adler's psychology of the individual in this context is then a failed heuristic tool for it is a discourse of medicalising science of the North Atlantic that was formulated to serve power and in the context of Martinique to serve hegemonic white power. To apply Adler's paradigm in any part of the neo-colonial world is then to affirm and ensure the sustainable hegemony of white power. Fanon continues on the contrasts between Adler's source of the neurosis and his as follows: "The Adlerian comparison embraces two terms; it is polarised by the ego. The Antillean comparison is surmounted by a third term: Its governing fiction is not personal but social." (Fanon 1977 pg. 215). Fanon expresses Adler's source as: Ego greater than The Other which comprises two terms Ego and The Other where Ego polarises the relationship to one of comparison making the Ego greater than The Other. For the Antillean comparison of Fanon, the Ego is different from The Other as there is no polarisation between Ego and The Other hence no comparison as the result of Ego polarisation. For both Ego and The Other are superseded, surmounted and dominated by a hegemonic third term: the pattern of the white man. The source of the neurosis is then social not personal. Fanon sums up his position as follows: "The Martinican is a man crucified. The environment that has shaped him (but that he has not shaped) has horribly drawn and quartered him, and he feeds this cultural environment with his blood and essences." (Fanon 1977 pg. 216). Fanon has found the source and has determined that the source is social but in its origin the Martinican has no impact on the source but it impacts the Martinican. The Martinican is the captive of the source and it is rooted in the cultural order, the cultural environment, the social order of Martinique. Clearly this cultural environment is rooted in the discourse of the Negro with a historical legacy from enslavement to the present.

Fanon indicates that if he were Adlerian he would have informed his friend/patient that in the pursuit of his desire to be a man, which is to be white, his neurosis, his psychic instability and the rupture of his ego were all the result of the governing fiction not the social order. As an Adlerian Fanon would then advise his friend/patient to accept the drawback, the blowback from his quest for manhood/whiteness for that is the price to be paid, hence it is necessary to accept the place assigned to his friend. Adler's paradigm is then averse to social change via individual action as it views the society as a totality which is more than the sum of the individuals. Adler's paradigm is then a discourse of medicalising science that is an instrument of power. Fanon rejects Adler's paradigm and states as follows: "Certainly not! I will not say that at all! I will tell him, 'The environment, society are responsible for your delusion.' Once that has been said, the rest will follow of itself, and that is what we know. The end of the world." (Fanon 1977 pg. 216). Adler's discourse is an instrument of power to ensure the sustainable hegemony of white power by refusing to see the social in the reality of the Negro, whilst Fanon's paradigm sole aim is to dismantle the world of sustainable white power by exposing its reality, impact and suffering unleashed on non-white peoples.

G.W. F. Hegel and Fanon

Fanon unlike his treatment of Adler presents a narrative on Hegel's discourse in the work "The Phenomenology of Mind", thereby avoiding a critique of the nature of what he did on Adler, of the work of a poster boy for the discourse of white supremacy and its subservient discourse of the Negro. Fanon in his narrative of Hegel is indicating the flaws of Hegel's discourse but it is up to the reader to find it in his narrative. Fanon's narrative commences with the issue of the other as follows: "Man is human only to the extent to which he tries to impose his existence on another man in order to be recognised by him. It is on that other being, on recognition by that other being, that his own human worth and reality depend." (Fanon 1977 pgs. 216-217). The basic premise is that without the other the human will not be human and will be alienated from the condition of being human. The human must dominate another human, constituting the other, where the dominant is showered with human recognition which determines the worth and reality of the dominant. If the other fails to impose, to dominate a human then the other is condemned to being an alienated, non-human other. The core question lies in the nature of the relation between the human seeking recognition from the other. Apparently Hegel does not factor power and domination into the relationship between human and other and the need and quest for recognition. What if the dominant is of a specific race whilst the other is of a different race, will the dominant race allow the dominated race to make them an Other? Clearly, from the outset Hegel's discourse is blind to power relations, power and a social order as it only sees deliberately the individual, specifically the white male individual with potency. Hence Hegel's blindness to colonial domination! Fanon continues: "There is not an open conflict between black and white.

One day the White Master, *without conflict*, recognised the Negro slave. But the former slave wants to *make himself* recognised." "Historically, the Negro steeped in the inessentiality of servitude was set free by his master. He did not fight for his freedom. Out of slavery the Negro burst into the lists where his master stood. The Negro has not become a master. Where there are no longer slaves, there are no longer masters. The Negro is a slave who has been allowed to assume the attitude of a master. The white man is a master who has allowed his slaves to eat at his table." (Fanon 1977 pgs. 217 and 219). For Hegel there was no conflict between black and white, specifically between massa and the enslaved, for massa under no compulsion recognised the slave. Massa then recognised the enslaved as human and made her/him the white man's other whereas before there was no such recognition, therefore the enslaved was sub-human, beast, animal/machine unfit to be massa's other. Massa then out of the innate superiority and humanity of his white consciousness finally recognised the African enslaved, made them his human other. Hegel's master race wields the power to define and award humanity through recognition at will without a hint of compulsion exerted and conflict between races. The former slave is now exerting upon the former massa the mechanism to have massa now be his other for such is the dialectical duality of recognition and Hegel has a grave problem with the process as the enslaved never fought for their freedom, it was gift from the white man. Thereby freeing the enslaved from servitude that rendered them inessential. But the inessential servitude was in the economic interests of massa and the metropole that exerted hegemony over her/him as this inessential servitude was part of a globalised geopolitical order under the hegemony of white North Atlantic folks. As with all racists Hegel is in denial. Hegel is insisting that the former enslaved must forever be thankful for the magnanimity of massa to end their enslavement, to the extent of being obligated. For you never fought for your freedom and power, and dominance resides in the hands of the white man in spite of the end of enslavement for massa allowed the slave to assume the attitude of the master and the slave to eat at the table of the massa. Massa wields power before and after the end of enslavement as the former enslaved wants to be massa but without slaves there can be no massa for massa erased the enslaved. With enslavement the Negro has failed to grasp the mechanism of recognition and the Other for freedom was a gift granted never fought for. Hegel is then framing the gravity of the mistake the white man made to recognise the enslaved African as a human by ending African enslavement. For this *recognition* did not match the existential reality of inessentiality as a result of servitude, which the enslaved African passively accepted and was a passive recipient of freedom at the hands of the white man. For Hegel the enslaved African was simply not worthy to now seek to be a massa through *recognition* of the humanity of the white man by imposing otherhood on the white man, for the humanity of the white man preceded the *recognition* of the enslaved African by the white man. Hegel is then a white supremacist. Fanon now deals with Hegel's dialectic as follows: "At the foundation of the Hegelian dialectic there is an absolute reciprocity which must be emphasised. It is in the degree to which I go beyond my own immediate being that I apprehended the existence of the other as a natural and more than natural reality. If I close the circuit, if I prevent the accomplishment of movement in two directions, I keep the other within himself. Ultimately, I deprive him even of this being-for-itself. (Fanon 1977 pg. 217). Hegel's dialectic is then driven by the needs of an absolute reciprocity, a totality founded on reciprocity where human interaction must be reciprocal in order to trigger this dialectic, thereby engaging the totality of reciprocity which results in the consciousness of being-for-itself. Hegel is insisting that humans can refuse reciprocal action, thereby stunting the development of the humans they refused to reciprocate with and themselves as the other remains trapped in the human and the consciousness of self is never attained. Fanon continues: "The only means of breaking this vicious circle that throws me back on myself is to restore to the other, through mediation and recognition, his human reality, which is different from natural reality. The other has to perform the same operation." (Fanon 1977 pg. 217). The African enslaved before the end of slavery was then in a natural state as there was no recognition and mediation to engage the other of the African enslaved, thereby constituting condition of having the other imprisoned within themselves, stunted and underdeveloped. The enslaved African was less than human as they were even deprived of the consciousness of being-for-itself. They simply had no consciousness of self, making them subhuman at best. The question for Hegel is how did the reciprocity emerge following the end of African enslavement in a social order where reducing the African to a natural state was the strategic aim of power in this social order and it worked for those wielding power? It never emerged for

Hegel's schema existed in Hegel's mind not on the ground in the colonial order of the West Indies. Fanon now deals with Hegel's concept of consciousness as follows: "In its immediacy, consciousness of self is simply being-for-itself. In order to win the certainty of oneself, the incorporation of the concept of recognition is essential. Similarly, the other is waiting for recognition by us, in order to burgeon into the universal consciousness of self." (Fanon 1977 pg. 217). Freedom for the formerly enslaved will only be real and meaningful when they experience consciousness of self, but to attain this condition they must now for the first time historically be recognised by the white man to awaken the other in both of them. In a state of freedom, the African is now driven by the need for recognition, for consciousness of self wants to be expanded to the universal consciousness of self and the refusal of recognition is restricting the flowering of the long mortified other. The clash between the other and self-consciousness generates desire which is the driving force of conflict in the clash between the recalcitrant other and self-consciousness. Fanon states: "Thus human reality in-itself-for-itself can be achieved only through conflict and through the risk that conflict implies." "He who is reluctant to recognise me opposes me. In a savage struggle I am willing to accept convulsions of death, invincible dissolutions, but also the possibility of the impossible." (Fanon 1977 pg. 218). Massa in keeping with Hegel's paradigm, could have only ended African enslavement without conflict because the enslaved were in a natural state devoid of consciousness of self and desire, hence subhuman at best. Which means that West Indian slave societies were not of the human world, a world of reciprocal recognitions as this non-human world was incapable of generating conflict as defined by Hegel's paradigm as there was no consciousness of self in its quest for totality of the universal in resistance against an unwilling other, hence no Hegelian desire was capable of being generated. What is the condition of not being a human world, is it being a West Indian slave society? Hegel's rant that the former African enslaved wants to make himself recognised is unfathomable within the ambit of his paradigm. For the former enslaved must now demand recognition if it is not forthcoming for the basis of recognition is a reciprocal flow according to Hegel. Hegel then has a problem with the demographic majority now making demands on the minority whites for he is seeing domination and all the paranoia generated by Negrophobia and the sexualised/genitalized Negro "Mandingo." Hegel's paradigm insists that it is only with a reciprocal flow of recognition will a human world emerge and develop in the former slave colonies and the most potent sign of this evolution is desire driving conflict. Apparently he has grave reservations of this process being unleashed in the West Indies, hence his position on the formerly enslaved Africans wanting to make themselves recognised, for when this recognition is given the flow begins and the process to realise the human world becomes unstoppable. Hegel was then fearful of his paradigm successfully applied to African dominated societies, being the white supremacist that he was, this was strictly a reality for whites only.

At this point in the text Fanon dumps the narrative mode and now goes into the attack in a prosecutory vein. Fanon states: "but then they decided to promote the machine-animal-men to the supreme rank of *men. Slavery shall no longer exist on French soil.*" "The upheaval reached the Negroes from without. The black man was acted upon. Values that had not been created by his actions, values that had not been born of the systolic tide of his blood...The upheaval did not make a difference in the Negro he went from one way of life to another, but not from one life to another." "so the announcement of the liberation of the black slaves produced psychoses and sudden deaths." (Fanon 1977 pg. 220). In his prosecutorial assault on Hegel, Fanon insists that these magnanimous white men/massa simply decided to now recognise the machine-animal-men of the enslaved African as men without due regard or consideration of the sustainability of massa's position of power in light of this action to now face free black people where massa is a demographic minority. The Negro was then in play as she/he was engulfed in upheaval, societal and personal, inundated under imposed white values therefore alien to his existential experience, cultural legacy and being. But the upheaval changed the way of life, not the life of the formerly enslaved Africans as the power relations remained the same in spite of being legally free people. Daily life did not match the legitimate expectations of free people as the way of life changed, but the life of free people was qualitatively worse than that of the enslaved for you were no longer the property of a massa but now free open game to be hunted by the State and all white people. As labour, tax payers, juridic subjects to enter into contracts and to be levied upon, therefore free to be normalised and policed by the State. Liberation then triggered psychoses and sudden deaths amongst the former enslaved Africans. For Fanon this issue is summed up as follows: "The white man, in the capacity of master, said to the Negro8, 'From now on you are free.'" (Fanon 1977 pg. 220). In the footnote to this line of the text Fanon states: "8 I hope I have shown that here the master differs basically from the master described by Hegel. For Hegel there is reciprocity; here the master laughs at the consciousness of the slave. What he wants from the slave is not recognition but work." (Fanon 1977 pg. 220). Fanon is insisting that the massa described in Hegel's paradigm does not exist in the reality of the power relation between massa and the African enslaved for there is no reciprocity between massa and the enslaved and formerly enslaved African. Massa does not want recognition from the formerly enslaved African, he rejects the consciousness of the African as what he wants is the labour of the African. Massa wants a servile African worker at the cost he determines and polices in conjunction with the State. Fanon continues: "In the same way, the slave here is in no way identifiable with the slave who loses himself in the object and finds in his work the source of his liberation. The Negro wants to be like the master. Therefore, he is less independent than the Hegelian slave. In Hegel the slave turns away from the master and turns toward the object. Here the slave turns toward the master and abandons the object." (Fanon 1977 pg. 220). Hegel's paradigm is addressing the abolition of slavery and the freeing of the African enslaved by massa, but the paradigm has no traction with the reality it is supposedly explaining on the ground. This absence of traction with reality on the ground, indicates that Hegel's paradigm is falsified by reality and it is actually manufacturing its own paradigmatic reality which will be imposed to silence reality on the ground especially expressions of the African. The enslaved of reality has no object to embrace, immerse himself in and through work finally finding liberation. This is not the objective reality of the former enslaved African as with freedom there is no object to grasp and immerse herself/himself in, there are only power relations of a colonial State and its social order defined and operationalised by a race hierarchy and white supremacy. Hegel's paradigm is then a discourse of power designed to ensure the sustainable hegemony of white power. The power relations demand that the formerly enslaved African cling to massa and strive to be like massa, thereby forming the basis of the drive to make yourself into an object of massa in subservience to white power.

Fanon continues: "But the Negro knows nothing of the cost of freedom, for he has not fought for it. From time to time he has fought for Liberty and Justice, but these were always white liberty and white justice; that is, values secreted by his masters." (Fanon 1977 pg. 221). Fanon responds to Hegel's position that the enslaved African received freedom as a gift from massa never having fought for it. Fanon insists that the enslaved African did fight for liberty and justice but it was always for white liberty and justice for the benefit of the white race not for the African, for white liberty and justice does not apply nor include the African and all other non-white races. The Haitian Revolution was fought for African liberty and justice, defined by African concepts of liberty and justice in a colony of the North Atlantic in the Western hemisphere. This African resurgence must then be incessantly assaulted as it challenges the discourse of the Negro hence the constant, sustainable war across time and space to erase the legacy, the event and the very historical fabric of the Haitian Revolution as it impacts the landscape of Haiti on a daily basis. The methodology of power utilised across time is the operationalised punishment of the African Haitian masses made possible by those of the Haitian elite plagued with hallucinatory whiteness in control of the Haitian State. Fanon posits that the white man responds to Negro aggression towards him in an attempt to disarm the Negro by insisting that there is no difference between white and black. Fanon states: "And yet the Negro *knows* there is a difference. He *wants* it. He wants the white man to turn on him and shout: 'Damn nigger.' But most often there is nothing-nothing but indifference, or a paternalistic-curiosity. The former slave needs a challenge to his humanity, he wants a conflict, a riot. But it is too late." (Fanon 1977 pg. 221)). All non-white persons know that there is a difference, for that is made potently clear to all of us who interact with white folks, but we also perceive and know our difference from them and would prefer that the chasm that divides and the hate that straddles the chasm be simply expressed openly rather than the smiles with the expectation of the blood to follow. We are then never at ease, always in expectation of the other shoe to drop which impacts our well-being. But what we want will never materialise as we are in a power relation where having surrendered by making ourselves an object, we are passive recipients of dominant power and we respond with masochism, neurosis, self-hate and self-immolation. For we are constantly seeking the approval of, seeking to please and perpetually in search of the normalisation of massa, to escape from the smiling faces that mask the race hate, the race hate devoid of smiling faces or whatever for what sums up our condition as a result of sustainable white hegemony: UNCERTAINTY! In closing this chapter Fanon on the French Negro states: "For the French Negro the situation is unbearable. Unbearable ever to be sure whether the white man considers him consciousness in-itself-for itself, he must forever absorb himself in uncovering resistance, opposition, challenge." (Fanon 1977 pg. 222). For all of us non-whites the existential condition is unbearable as we are never certain and convinced that we are viewed as being human as the white man. Ever suspicious, ever anxious, ever plagued by expectations of actions that illustrate our inhumanity, including the Final Solution, we adopt a spectrum of responses and survival strategies that enhance and embolden the attack and our attackers. We are then condemned to the perpetual quest for resistance, opposition and challenge as liberation appears as a fleeting illusion. The reason for this is the methodology of resistance chosen and embraced for there can be no liberation via the hegemonic discourse of the white man, only uncertainty and crucifixion.

Fanon ends the chapter with this statement: "To educate man to be *actional,* preserving in all his relations his respect for the basic values that constitute a human world, is the prime task of him who, having taken thought, prepare to act." (Fanon 1977 pg. 222). The issue now is to act strategically, and to do this demands education to be actional which must be an alternative form of education we are permitted under the sustainable hegemony of white supremacy. For under white supremacy we are educated to be dominated, passive, hand wringers and racist, especially to non-whites. Action education demands an alternate discourse, worldview, paradigm and cosmology that roots us in human values for a human world that shares the Earth with a diversity of non-human life. Education for action, action for liberation cannot be cobbled together from a copy and paste of the white man's discourse, for without the hard work undertaken to build the alternate paradigm, discourse and worldview all attempts at liberation will be still born. Fanon's text deconstructed was one such contribution to the erection of the alternate education for action, giving birth to action for liberation. The reality is that in the second decade of the 21st century Fanon's contribution remains relevant as the alternate education for action is presently under grave assault whilst still in a condition of being incomplete.

Chapter 9
Fanon's Conclusions

Alienation, Resistance and the Past

Fanon insists that the disalienation of a doctor of medicine born in Guadeloupe and that of a labourer in Abidjan are fundamentally different as the motivations involved in both cases are basically different. Fanon states: "In the first case, the alienation is of an almost intellectual character. Insofar as he conceives of European culture as a means of stripping himself of his race, he becomes alienated. In the second case, it is a question of a system based on the exploitation of a given race by another, on the contempt in which a branch of humanity is held by a form of civilisation that pretends to superiority." (Fanon 1977 pgs. 223-224). Fanon has posited two instances of alienation that are materially different requiring two different strategies that address the distinct realities of both states. The first case is the instance of the need to whiten oneself driven by the embrace of the imposed culture resulting in alienation. The second case is the exploitation of a race, its labour power by an inherently superior dominant race where the point of impact is the exploitation of labour justified by manifest destiny. There is then the possibility of two instances of alienation in this case: the alienation of labour power and the alienation of race. To address only a single form of alienation in this case impacts the power relation where it evolves into extremes. Fanon now switches to his philosophical conclusions as follows: "I do not carry innocence to the point of believing that appeals to reason or to respect for human dignity can alter reality." (Fanon 1977 pg. 224). Fanon insists that he is cognisant and appreciative of the operational reality of change and the possibility of change. There must then be an operational methodology that impacts reality to enable change. Fanon then insists that for the Negro sugar plantation worker in Le Robert the only solution is to fight and the sugar worker is conscious of this reality and will embark upon it and will pursue it: "because he cannot conceive of life otherwise than in the form of a battle against exploitation, misery, and hunger." (Fanon 1977 pg. 224). Fanon is accurate in this position for all power generates resistance but resistance to power wears you down, exhausts you, for hegemonic power must deflect resistance as it perpetually threatens sustainable hegemony. Those who then must fight but command the barest of resources for a long term battle are then recipients of the gravest pressure by hegemonic power to surrender, but even in surrender there is resistance. The lesson is there is no revolutionary class, race or group who by a propensity and a predilection will make the revolution. The only commonality is the pressing need to fight, to resist, how we operationalise this resistance is the grave issue. Fanon continues on this theme by speaking of the black working class people he encountered in Paris who: "never took it on themselves to pose the problem of the discovery of a Negro past. They knew they were black, but, they told me, that made no difference in anything. In which they were absolutely right." (Fanon 1977 pg. 224). The fact of blackness where black is a given and the prime reality is survival through resistance. For the Negro past is not a necessity to resistance and survival, for it is a given, and a problem for those who have rejected their race and embraced whiteness. Posing the problem of the Negro past is then a mechanism fashioned by hallucinatory whiteness to paralyse resistance via handwringing inertia, otherwise originally conceptualised as shucking and jiving your black self and other non-whites. Fanon states: "Like it or not, the past can in no way guide me in the present moment." (Fanon 1977 pg. 225). The imperative for resistance operationalised by a driving strategy in the present, here and now can only be organically linked to a relevant past where this past is operationally and strategically relevant to today, now, the present. The past can then be the terrain of retreat, of shucking and jiving ourselves to rationalise our impotence. Fanon states: "The discovery of the existence of a Negro civilisation in the fifteenth century confers no patent of humanity on me." (Fanon 1977 pg. 225). The search for affirmation of our humanity by delving into pasts that we configure to aid and abet our agenda to shuck and jive ourselves and our races. To search for a patent of humanity potently illustrates the embrace of the inferiority complex driven by the desire to be white at all costs. There is no resistance, there is only the desire for whiteness and affirmation which means that there is no commitment, no morality, no respect and no gratitude to stand in the way of this desire. In the quest for whiteness nothing is sacred, nothing is prohibited - you sell your family, your race and yourself down the river for a mess of white pottage. There can be no resistance from those as these who insist to us that our terrain of action is the past for they are selling us chains, white chains.

Fanon continues on the past: "The Negro, however sincere, is the slave of the past. Face to face with the white man, the Negro has a past to legitimate, a vengeance to exact; face to face with the Negro, the contemporary white man feels the need to recall the times of cannibalism." (Fanon 1977 pg. 225). The power relation with the white man enslaves the Negro in the past constructed by the hegemonic white order thereby trapping the Negro in the landscape of the need for compulsive legitimation of their past. This enslavement in a past constructed by the hegemonic white supremacist order drives the need to confront the white man, the quest for vengeance, whilst in the face off of two races the white man responds with memories framed by a constructed black past of the threat posed to the white race by the cannibal. Never eat a white meat yet! Under the hegemony of white supremacy there can only be extremism borne out of alienation. Fanon now insists that the problem is time as follows: "The problem considered here is one of time. Those Negroes and white men will be disalienated who refuse to let themselves be sealed away in the materialised Tower of the Past. For many other Negroes, in other ways, as disalienation will come into being through their refusal to accept the present as definitive." (Fanon 1977 pg. 226). Disalienation is possible via two paths specifically with the manner in which the past and present are conceptualised and approached. To reject the past as definitive and defining of the present ensures the possibility of disalienation as the use of a mythic past to define and justify the order of the present that is the terrain of alienation. The other path calls for the rejection of the present as definitive, unchanging, linear reality, the product of truth and science. Both the Tower of the Past and the Present as definitive are instruments of power designed to ensure the sustainability of the hegemonic white supremacist order. Deep interrogation of the discourse of the past and present are then necessary to expose their linear, mythic historico-political scientific discourses of white supremacist power. Fanon insists: "I will not make myself the man of any past. I do not want to exalt the past at the expense of my present and my future." (Fanon 1977 pg. 226). The past must serve the present and future which are rooted in the quest for and attainment of disalienation. This past has then to be strategically constructed to root and serve the quest for disalienation which means that a past has to be formulated and defined that counters our past constituted by white supremacist discourse through deconstruction and the construction of our alternate past. To exalt the mythic past formulated for us by white supremacist discourse is to deny our future and present as self-determining humans. Fanon then presents his potent example of his position on the past as follows: "The Vietnamese who die before the firing squads are not hoping that their sacrifices will bring about the reappearance of a past. It is for the sake of the present and of the future that they are willing to die." (Fanon 1977 pg. 227). Fanon's example is drawn from the war for independence waged by the Vietnamese against French colonial domination of Vietnam with specific reference to Vietnamese who chose to die at the hands of the French colonial firing squads in the quest for liberation in the present and for a free future. Vietnamese willingly chose death rather than subservience to white French colonial domination, the ultimate personal sacrifice for the present and the future, not for a past which denies the present and the future desired. But for their present and future which defines the necessary past. This is the dynamic of present, future and defined past Fanon demands.

Fanon continues on the weight of the Past and the threats posed as follows: "Moral anguish in the face of the massiveness of the past? I am a Negro and tons of chains, storms of blows, rivers of expectoration flow down my shoulders. But I do not have the right to allow myself to bog down. I do not have the right to allow the slightest fragment to remain in my existence. I do not have the right to allow myself to be mired in what the past has determined. I am not the slave of the Slavery that dehumanised my ancestors." (Fanon 1977 pg. 230). The Past can bog down, immerse the Negro of the present with moral anguish but what right do I have to immobile myself, to paralyse all intent to action and the pursuit and exercise of freedom by languishing in the Past when I am not a slave of the slavery of the Past. The Past threatens paralysis via the immersion in victimhood for there is no grasp of and the exercise of freedom whilst immersed in the paralysis of victimhood characterised by persistent hand wringing. The Past has to be exorcised as it is formulated as the stumbling block to freedom for it is an instrument of power designed to create subservience, servility and abnormality. Fanon states: "The body of history does not determine a single one of my actions. I am my own foundation. And it is by going beyond the historical, instrumental hypothesis that I will initiate the cycle of my freedom." (Fanon 1977 pg. 231). Fanon has now liberated himself from the bondage of the history that is an instrument of power, this historical, instrumental hypothesis that insists it is the science of history, which is a discourse of power designed to problematize its strategic target. Fanon has then to strategically respond by establishing himself as his own foundation which enables the grasp and exercise of freedom. As it is simply the manufactured realities of white power designed to problematize and abnormalise when you reject its power, presence and truth, your path to freedom is now realisable provided you do want the uncertainty of freedom. Fanon ends his discourse of the Past as follows: "The disaster of the man of colour lies in the fact that he was enslaved. The disaster and inhumanity of the white man lie in the fact that somewhere he has killed man. And even today they subsist, to organise this dehumanisation rationally. But I as a man of colour, to the extent that it becomes possible to exist absolutely, do not have the right to lock myself into a world of retroactive reparations." (Fanon 1977 pg. 231). The disasters of the man of colour and the white man are both strategically necessary to this rational dehumanisation for the white man cannot successfully accomplish this task without his willing accomplice, the man of colour. A man of colour who has grasped freedom by ceasing to be an accomplice to rational dehumanisation and abnormalisation and is now seeking to live a life rooted in absolute self-determination and self-definition have abrogated the right granted to the abnormal to be locked in a world where you perpetually desire and seek out reparations locked and grounded in the past never the present. The very concept of reparations illustrates the demand for inclusion into the white world and to be finally accepted as a fitting part of the white world given our complicity with the white racist hegemonist discourse and agenda. The call for amends, reparations involves being locked in the Past and the refusal to accept complicity in the process, for the claim is the product of victimhood and claims of innocence.

Middle Class Society

Fanon now presents his position on what he defines as middle class society and all its dysfunctionalities as follows: "Intellectual alienation is a creation of middle class society. What I call middle class society is any society that becomes rigidified in predetermined forms, forbidding all evolution, all gains, all progress, all discovery. I call middle class society a closed society in which life has no taste, in which the air is tainted, in which ideas and men are corrupt. And I think a man who takes a stand against this death is in a sense a revolutionary." (Fanon 1977 pgs. 224-225). One product of middle class society is intellectual alienation where this closed, inward looking, incestuous social order alienates humankind from her/his intellectual capacity. Where corrupt ideas wielded by corrupt humans destroy the creativity, the life, the dynamic of humankind trapped in the social order of middle class society. Intellectual alienation is then death, and to resist this death is a revolutionary action, for middle class society is driven by extremes of human action on humans, nonhuman life and the ecosystem.

The Negro/the Black man and the White man

Fanon presents his conclusions on the Negro as follows: "I have ceaselessly striven to show the Negro that in a sense he makes himself abnormal; to show the white man that he is at once the perpetrator and victim of a delusion." (Fanon 1977 pg. 225). The white man perpetuates a delusion of the inferiority of the Negro and by believing and acting upon his delusion he is a victim of his delusion. Whilst the target of the delusion ensures the strategic potency and viability of the delusion by making himself abnormal. The delusion is an instrument of power, framed and deployed with strategic intent but the target of the attack is not a passive recipient, a victim as the Negro/Black must make themselves abnormal by accepting and acting upon this white assault. There is then a point of resistance to power present at the point of contact and intersection where the Negro has a choice of action to accept and apply the attacking discourse or to resist. There are then no victims, just willing accomplices or soldiers of resistance in an engagement. Fanon is then describing a power relation driven by the quest for white racist hegemony and the terrain of choices available to the target, the Negro/Black. The other aspect of the power relation of Fanon is the impact of the power relation on whites where the acceptance, belief and action arising from the delusion is in fact a power relation, an instrument of power towards normalisation and social control. Fanon continues: "The black man wants to be like the white man. For the black man there is only one destiny. And it is white. Long ago the black man admitted the unarguable superiority of the white man, and all his efforts are aimed at achieving a white existence." (Fanon 1977 pg. 228). With the surrender to the discourse of white supremacy by black people there can be only one destiny and that is to be white, but the black man can never be epidermically white. To surrender to the white supremacist discourse leads to one path where you pursue frantically a condition that is unattainable, hence the need for chemical and surgical transformation of the epidermis and other expressions of race characteristics. The Negroes are then consigned to languish in a netherworld manufactured for the bastard children of Sisyphus. Fanon expresses this reality as follows: "My life is caught in the lasso of existence. My freedom turns me back on myself. No, I do not have the right to be a Negro. I do not have the duty to be this or that...If the white man challenges my humanity I will impose my whole weight as a man on his life and show him that I am not that 'sho' good eatin'" that he persists in imagining." (Fanon 1977 pg. 229). Fanon's lasso of existence is the futile circularity that results from being defined by, accepting and acting upon the discourse of white supremacy where we are constituted as contradictions that cannot resolve themselves. Freedom is circular as we are in an illusory state of freedom for ourselves that render us in bondage to white supremacist discourse, where Negrohood is bestowed on us by dint of our subservience, for it is not our creation but that of white supremacist discourse. For our ancestors loaded on the slave ships became Negroes, before that signal event the Negro had no specificity in Africa. We are then always compelled to measure ourselves against the yardstick of white racism for we are always challenged by white hegemony and we are always compelled to anger as we repeatedly strive to indicate over and over that we are not shucking and jiving niggers. A circularity of futility for white folks can never be impressed with such protests to change the hegemonic white supremacist discourse, for they are also being constituted by the instruments of power of this racist discourse and they are content with and luxuriate in the perception that they wield power over us, as that is the salve spread over the raw wounds that demand resistance. The difference then is power and hegemony enjoyed as a race and denied to other races, where the dominated is burdened to perpetually prove their humanity but only to themselves as the dominant race insists that the inherent inferiority of the dominated is a scientific fact, a done deal. Non-white races caught in this futile circularity are then shoring up their servility by repeatedly shouting their humanity to a deaf master race! This is then an act to persuade yourself to ensure that you are sustainably servile, eschewing the need for resistance. Fanon states the counter position as follows: "I have one right alone: That of demanding human behaviour from the other. One duty alone: That of not renouncing my freedom through my choices. I have no wish to be the victim of the *Fraud* of a black world. My life should not be devoted to drawing up the balance sheet of Negro values. There is no white world, there is no white ethic, any more than there is a white intelligence." (Fanon 1977 pg. 229). The only right Fanon has is to demand human behaviour from the white and black races for both form the other and he can exercise this single right only when he executes his duty of clasping his freedom by not exercising the choice to make himself abnormal, to surrender thereby foregoing resistance. To demand his right and to exercise his freedom, frees Fanon from the fraud perpetuated by the concept of a black world, for a black world is the construct of white hegemonic power as black exists only in relation to white. Fanon's life will then be free of the chains of forever having to assert the humanity of the Negro in the face of white racism, constantly accounting for all that proves the humanity of the Negro, forever trapped in a futile dance of circularity that changes nothing. Fanon is free of the black/white duality driven by the discourse of hegemonic white supremacy where he can now assert that there is no white world, white intelligence and white ethic which in the dance of the duality must be extended to no black world, no black intelligence and no black ethic there is only the world, the Earth, human intelligence and human ethics. From linear singularity expressed as a racist totality to a cyclical multiverse driven by diverse humanity in a time/space continuum. To accept a white world, white intelligence and white ethic you in turn embrace black on black racism and extremism and the Final Solution. Fanon continues: "I, the man of colour, want only this: That the tool never possesses the man. That the enslavement of man by man by man cease forever. That is, of one by another. That it be possible for me to discover and to love man, wherever he may be. The Negro is not. Any more than the white man.

Both must turn their backs on the inhuman voices which were those of their respective ancestors in order that authentic communication be possible. Before it can adopt a positive voice, freedom requires an effort at disalienation. It is through the effort to recapture the self and to scrutinise the self, it is through the lasting tension of their freedom that men will be able to create the ideal conditions of existence for a human world." (Fanon 1977 pg. 231). The entire process hinges on disalienation for without it there can be no freedom to realise the strategic ends Fanon lists at the beginning of the quotation, only freedom to make ourselves abnormal, objects of white power. Without disalienation freedom can never evolve into a positive voice, it will never evolve into the free terrain necessary to create the human world. The world driven by imperialist, racist capitalist power will continue with its expressions of exploitation and a diversity of hate and extremism expressed as human action. This specific world is not human but a world of alienated humans which makes it impossible to attain Fanon's wishes where the product of human hands does not command the human, that the exploitation of man by man through various systems of enslavement cease for all times and most of all where humanity can now love all humanity as there is no distinction, exclusion and hierarchical differentiation. This is only attainable when the inhuman voices of the past are silenced and new voices and new communications of inclusion that embrace difference emancipated from dual totalities become hegemonic. Fanon ends his conclusions as follows: "Why not the quite simple attempt to touch the other, to feel the other, to explain the other to myself? Was my freedom not given to me then in order to build the world of the You?" "My final prayer: O my body, make of me always a man who questions!" (Fanon 1977 pgs. 231-232). The human who perpetually questions is necessary towards accomplishing the task of recapturing the self from The Other whose discursive task is to twist, distort and abnormalise the self so necessary to servility. The self must be scrutinised to be purged of its abnormality, but to facilitate scrutiny, renovation and refurbishment it has to be recaptured from The Other. The Other and the other have then to be dismantled by dealing with, reaching out to and explaining the You to self. The Other must no longer define the You as the other, thereby placing the soul of identity, meaning and definition over the You occluding the You with power, power relations and the quest for hegemony and subservience. The You must speak for itself and be understood and accepted for itself, thereby enabling the human world of the You, not the abnormal world of The Other, its other, race hate, racist supremacy, alienation and abnormality.

Chapter 10
The Duality of the Arab and the White Man

To ensure a complete deconstruction of Fanon's discourse presented in "Black Skin White Masks" articles of Fanon collected and published after his death as "Toward the African Revolution" that expressed this discourse of Fanon will be deconstructed in this work.

The "North African Syndrome" (First published 1952 in French)

Fanon in 1952 published this article dealing with the Arab migrants to France and the nature of the power relationship between white and Arab in France. This is a fitting addition to the discourse of "Black Skin White Masks" which primarily focused on the African Antillean in the Antilles and France.

Fanon defines his task in the article as follows: "I want to show in what is to follow that, in the specific case of the North African who has emigrated to France, a theory of inhumanity is in a fair way to finding its laws and its corollaries." Who are they, in truth, those creatures who hide, who are hidden by social truth beneath the attributes of bicot, bounioule, arabe, raton, sidi, mon z'ami?" (Fanon 1969 pgs. 3-4). Fanon insists that there is a social truth that hides and masks the Arab in France, by, via, through and expressed by racist expressions which illustrate the Arab soul affixed to the body of the Arab as bicot, arabe, bounioule, raton, sidi and mon z'ami. There is then a theory of inhumanity at work, operationalised and this discourse can be located and deconstructed by finding and locating its laws and corollaries. There is then a social structure, a social order in France that targets the Arab as an object of assault and discrimination.

Fanon then presents his thesis one dealing with the North African as follows: *"FIRST THESIS-That the behaviour of the North African often causes a medical staff to have misgivings as to the reality of his illness."* "Except in urgent cases...the North African arrives enveloped in vagueness." "You must not ask for specific symptoms: you would not be given any." "This conformity to the categories of time is something to which the North African seems to be hostile." "It is as though it is an effort for him to go back to where he no longer is. The past for him is a burning past. What he hopes is that he will never suffer again, never again be face to face with that past. The present pain, which visually mobilises the muscles of his face, suffices him." (Fanon 1969 pg. 4). What is this burning past that the Arab in France seeking medical intervention refuses to recall its memories of pain? What is the existential reality of this burning past whilst the Arab is living in France that she/he is willing to bear and accept pain in a sacrifice to evade the pain of the burning past? Fanon says there are two possible outcomes to this visit namely, the patient returns after a period of time complaining of the pain or the patient goes elsewhere in search of treatment. On the first possible outcome Fanon says as follows: "He *is* pain and he refuses to understand any language, and it is not far from the conclusion: It is because I am Arab that they don't treat me like others." (Fanon 1969 pg.5). The patient returns still in pain for he is pain and there is no medical relief, for relief is not the issue as the patient is not willing to abide by the medical instructions given. The patient soon comes to the conclusion that the ineffective treatment afforded by the medical establishment is as a result of being Arab. There is then a race dynamic, an expectation of discrimination, a power relation in which the Arab is in a position of being dominated by the white man. Fanon presents on this reality of the Arab as follows: "The North African's pain, for which we can find no lesional basis, is judged to have no consistency, no reality. Now the North African is a-man-who-doesn't-like work. So that whatever he does will be interpreted *a priori* on the basis of this." (Fanon 1969 pg. 6). This North African pain that has no explanation, for within the North Atlantic discourse of the science of medicine hence it has no materiality, consistency most of all no reality. This pain is then the product of the soul that has been formulated and drapes the body of the Arab defining the Arab for power and by power whereby the Arab is a bum, a layabout, lazy, shiftless and a shirker perpetually formulating excuses to evade work. From the initial contact between the Arab and the medical establishment this soul of the Arab, driven by the white supremacist discourse of the Arab is driving the interaction. Pain without a lesional basis is immediately placed on the perceptual radar screen of the medical establishment as the Arab is a-man-who-does-not-like to-work! This soul attached to all Arabs, impacts and determines the quality and nature of the interactions the Arab is part of in France during her/his lifespan. There is then a discourse of the Arab in France, distinct and separate from the discourse of the Negro, all under the hegemony of the discourse of white supremacy. The memories of the burning past of the Arab then flow out from European colonial conquest and domination as in the case of Algeria with French colonial conquest and domination. This burning past is encapsulated in the instruments of power unleashed on Arabs to constitute willing servile Arabs, summed up in the concepts of bicot, arabe, bounioule etc. with the reality of being a bicot minority in France of major concern to Fanon's task of analysis. Fanon comes to a conclusion on the North African with reference to his first thesis as follows: "In the face of this pain without lesion, this illness distributed in and over the whole body, this continuing suffering, the easiest attitude, to which one comes more or less rapidly, is the negative of any morbidity. When you come down to it, the North African is a simulator, a liar, a malingerer, a sluggard, a thief." (Fanon 1969 pg. 7). The behaviour of the North African/the bicot is abnormal as the pain he presents with has no connection to a physical morbidity but alternately he is not psychosomatic for the discourse of the Arab insists that he is morally abnormal, flawed, a perpetual, willing, conscious, practicing miscreant for he is bicot. The Arab is a bicot as he is a self-fulfilling prophecy as she/he simply cannot help themselves for they are morally retarded. Fanon's first thesis exposes the reality that white racism expressed through the discourse of the Arab and its instrument of power of the bicot, constitutes the perceptions of the Arab by the medical establishment and the nature of the actions taken and the manner in which the Arab patient presents his suffering to the white medical establishment. Simply one example of the white /Arab power relation in France.

Fanon's second thesis: "SECOND THESIS-That the attitude of medical personnel is very often an a priori attitude. The North African does not come with a substratum common to his race but on a foundation built by the European. In other words, the North African spontaneously, by the very fact of appearing on the scene, enters into a pre-existing framework." (Fanon 1969 pg. 7). With his entry into any space in France the Arab encounters the reality that she/he has been defined and assigned behavioural and mental characteristics with specific expectations attached, even though this was a space devoid of Arab entry and interaction before her/his entry. There is then a framework that exists and is operationally active without the need for interaction with Arabs to be operationalised or effective, for it is working on the worldview of non-Arabs, especially white folks in France. What is noteworthy here is the potent black on black racism that emerges from this discourse of the Arab, this pre-existing framework which effectively divides the non-white races in spaces under white hegemony. This discourse of the Arab, in its medicalised scientific flow, constructs the paradigm of the North African syndrome which problematizes the Arab and her/his pain. Fanon states: "The North African syndrome. The North African today who goes to see a doctor bears the deadweight of all his compatriots." "The pathology invented by the Arab does not interest us. It is a pseudo-pathology. The Arab is a pseudo-invalid. Every Arab is a man who suffers from an imaginary ailment. The young doctor or the young student who has never seen a sick Arab knows (the old medical tradition testifies to it) that 'those fellows are humbugs.'" (Fanon 1969 pgs. 8-9). The North African syndrome conditions the nature and manner in which white people, white medical personnel will interpret and act upon the ailment an Arab presents with, even in cases where they have never interacted with an Arab before. The discourse of the Arab insists that the Arab is a pseudo-invalid who presents with pseudo-pathologies which is the North African syndrome, not the nature of perception and interpretation and the manner of treatment afforded the Arab by white medical science. The soul with a multiplicity of definitions, mannerisms, peculiarities and behaviours that drapes the body of the Arab constitutes the syndrome as simply one of many instruments of power by which to normalise the Arab in the white dominated social order of France. The Arab impacted by the syndrome responds by insisting that simply being an Arab impacts the quality of medical care afforded her/him. Whilst there is the white North African syndrome where the white afflicted with the syndrome sees no need to gaze upon the Arab to uncover the reality of what constitutes the Arab, for white folks are comfortable with the North African syndrome and act upon it. They are then constituted by the white soul that drapes their body where the syndrome is an instrument of power to normalise white folks. Fanon continues: "The medical staff discovers the existence of a North African syndrome. Not experimentally, but on the basis of an oral tradition. The North African takes his place in this asymptomatic syndrome and is automatically put down as undisciplined (cf. medical discipline), inconsequential (with reference to the law according to which every symptom implies a lesion), and insincere (he says he is suffering when we know there are no *reasons* for suffering)." (Fanon 1969 pgs. 9-10). Fanon insists that the syndrome is a discourse, an oral tradition of French medical science which brands the Arab as undisciplined, inconsequential and insincere, as defined by Western and French medical science discourse, thereby amounting to the asymptomatic syndrome that afflicts the Arab. The Arab is constantly in pain without symptoms, which conditions the interaction between Arab and medical personnel as the Arab simply cannot be taken seriously.

The third thesis of Fanon is as follows: "THIRD THESIS-That the greatest willingness, the purest of intentions require enlightenment. Concerning the necessity of making a situational diagnosis." (Fanon 1969 pg. 10). Fanon is now seeking and presenting instances of what is offered as enlightenment on the Arab in this his third thesis. In this section of the text he refers to specific works critically exposing the nature of the enlightenment they contain and their rationale seeking to confirm the need for situational analysis. Fanon refers to a work by E Stern on psychosomatic medicine which is drawn from the oeuvre of Heinrich Meng whereby Fanon is using the Stern paradigm to determine the "situation" of the Arab in France which will then amount to a "situational diagnosis" in keeping with the paradigm of Meng necessary to exposing the efficacy of this paradigm. The first instance of the "situation" is the relations an Arab has with his associates. Fanon's position on this is as follows: "Is there not something a little comical about speaking of the North African's relations with his associates, in France? Does he *have* relations? Does he *have* associates? Is he not alone?" "From time to time one sees them working at some building, but one does not see them, one perceives them, one gets a glimpse of them. Associates? Relations? There are no contracts. There are only bumps. Do people realise how much that is gentle and polite is contained in this word 'contact'? Are there contacts? Are there relation?" (Fanon 1969 pgs. 10-11). Fanon is insisting that the Arab is a ghost in the French social order as she/ he is seen and perceived but without the gaze fixed upon her/him resulting in glimpses of them. There are then no associates of the Arabs of France, hence no relations and relationships with associates, there are then no contacts, no civil human interactions just bumps where humans in forced unavoidable contact mediate such contact through aggressive stances and language. There is nothing gentle and polite in these forced unavoidable contacts, which problematizes the Stern/Meng paradigm and its methodology of situational diagnosis. I personally experienced the nature of contact between Arabs and white folks in Lille, France in 2001 noting the level of hostility and aggression that was common to simple contact on the streets of Lille. The level of common hostility potently illustrated the race hate that pervades the social order. The second situation of the Stern/Meng is occupation and preoccupation where Fanon insists that the Arab is preoccupied with finding and retaining her/his job and he has no preoccupation. Fanon states: "He works, he is busy, he busies himself, he is kept busy. His preoccupations? I think the word does not exist in his language." (Fanon 1969 pg. 11). The third situation is sexuality where Fanon points to the discourse of the Arab and the impact on the Stern/Meng methodology and the results of a study utilising this methodology. As to the nature of Arab, sexuality defined by the discourse of the Arab, Fanon chooses as his example a doctoral thesis in medicine by Leon Mugniery. Mugniery insists that the Arab in France has a predisposition to consort with prostitutes, to choose to associate with prostitutes and to marry or co-inhabit with prostitutes and this is driven by their powerful sexual appetite which is the genetic predisposition of Arabs. The powerful sex drive of Arabs then poses a grave threat to white women and the purity of the race. The propensity to consort with prostitutes and to partake in homosexual sexuality illustrate the moral infirmity of the Arab and the threat posed to the white race by this morally deficient, sexually charged non-white race. The Arab presents a grave, complex threat to the white race and its social order. Above all, the Arab is a rapist intent on raping on a sustainable basis both genders of the white race. The Arab then presents a grave, potent threat to French civilisation as the Arab is a primitive, sexually driven brute devoid of the ability to create a civilisation as France and devoid of the experience of living in a civilisation comparable to that of France. To welcome this cretin to France and then grant them citizenship poses a grave threat to the future of French white civilisation. On this Fanon states: "Need anything be added?" (Fanon 1969 pg. 12). What is now apparently clear is that the Stern/Meng methodology is not geared to generate a "situational diagnosis", but to complement an instrument of biopower intent on normalising the Arab minority in France for the situations enumerated have no traction with the daily existential reality of the Arab in France. The fourth situation is the Arab's inner tension. Fanon's position on this situation is as follows: "Utterly unrealistic! You might as well speak of the inner tension of a stone. Inner tension indeed! What a joke!" (Fanon 1969 pg. 12). The fourth situation is for Fanon totally ridiculous and irrelevant to the Arab in France, further illustrating the fact that the situation methodology is an instrument of biopower by which to problematize the Arab, opening the path to normalisation. The fifth situation is the Arab's sense of security or insecurity. Fanon states: "The North African is in a perpetual state of insecurity. A multisegmented insecurity. The North African is never sure. The North African on the threshold of the French Nation-which is, we are told, his as well-experiences in the political realm, on the plane of citizenship, an imbroglio which no one is willing to face." (Fanon 1969 pgs. 12-13). The Arab is immersed in insecurity that is multisegmented, even multidimensional, which renders the Arab unsure, uncertain and apprehensive which reflects the reality of the imbroglio in the political realm that impacts the Arab in France where the belonging of the Arab to France, the welcoming of France to the Arab and the certainty that citizenship of France must bring to the Arab is never a certainty, a given as it remains constantly elusive. The space afforded the Arab in France is then forever plagued by uncertainty, by fluidity, by its transitory nature, by being unwelcome, forever an alien, a migrant, transitory, a subject of internal colonialism. This existential condition must impact the North African and their interaction with the French medical services. The sixth situation is the dangers that threaten the Arab and Fanon's position is as follows: "Threatened in his affectivity, threatened in his social activity, threatened in his membership in the community-the North African combines all the conditions that make a sick man." (Fanon 1969 pg. 13). The Arab in the French social order is then faced with assaults on her/his membership, belonging and place in the social order combined with assaults on her/his social activity and on the very humanity and potency of their being in the world. The discourse of the Arab with its instruments of biopower are then insisting to the Arab that they are less than human, presenting grave threats to the white social order and civilisation and are demanding that the Arab be normalised whilst occupying the space allocated to them as less than humans: the banlieues. This assault on the Arab has then impacted the health of the Arab as follows: "the first encounter with himself will occur in a neurotic mode, in a pathological mode; he will feel himself emptied, without life, in a bodily struggle with death, a death on this side of death, a death in life." (Fanon 1969 pg. 13). The Arab is neurotic, for that is the manner to deal with the existential reality of self for he is dead in life. This is the source of the pain that plagues the Arab that simply cannot be lesional in origin or expressed in the requisite French medical science manner to the doctors necessary for them to make sense of it, for their existential reality of self is not the Arab reality. The seventh and final solution is the evolution and story of his life, which Fanon says is not a story of the life of the Arab but of their death. Fanon states: "It would be better to say the history of his death. A daily death." (Fanon 1969 pg. 13). At the end of analysis of the seven "solutions" of the Stern/Meng schema it is painfully obvious that it has no relevance to the daily existential reality of the Arab in France dumped in the holding bays of the banlieues, a grim reminder of the Warsaw ghetto before the Final Solution.

Fanon describes the suffocating nature of the space allocated to the Arab in the French social order, a suffocating premium on space summed up and expressed by the banlieues, but these are spaces for normalisation and storage of non-whites, the internal colonies of Europe. Fanon states: "Where they find no room where you leave them no room where there is absolutely no room for them and you dare tell me it doesn't concern you! That it's no fault of yours! (Fanon 1969 pg. 14). Hence all space is at a premium for the Arab, for all space is under the hegemony of the instruments of biopower which are assaulting the Arab in all spaces to normalise them but the banlieues are specially designated spaces for Arabs as the pressure exerted in spaces are to entice them to embrace the banlieues, to consider them their spaces and to relentlessly move to redefine them as Arab spaces, which enhances hegemonic biopower's normalising assault on Arabs. Fanon then presents his most potent statement of the article under review as follows: "This man whom you thingify by calling him systematically Mohammed, whom you reconstruct, or rather whom you dissolve, on the basis of an idea, an idea you know to be repulsive (you know perfectly well you rob him of something, that something for which not so long ago you were ready to give up everything, even your life) well, don't you have the impression that you are emptying him of his substance?" (Fanon

1969 pg. 14). Under the assault of white supremacist discourse the Arab is dissolved and replaced with the THING called and summed up by the term Mohammed, which has now been redefined since the September 2001 attacks on the USA and thereafter. The idea that is the basis of the assault is white supremacy in defence of the white French homeland and its civilisation in the face of the grave threats posed by the Arab in France and Europe. The strategy calls for the Arab threat dissolved through reconstructing the Arab into a neurotic, socially suffocated, cloistered minority locked away in the banlieues. The key instrument is the denial of space towards the suffocation of Arabs that destroys their affectivity as a human in a social order.

Fanon now deals with the position that the Arab can stay where they belong as they are in our country namely a white country France as follows: "The trouble is; they have been told they were French. They learnt it in school. In the street. In the barracks. On the battlefields. They have had France squeezed into them wherever, in their bodies and in their souls, there was room for something apparently great." (Fanon 1969 pg. 15). French colonial domination in North Africa for the sake of colonial hegemony insisted that the Arab was French and hammered that into the colonised in an attempt to render the Arab pliant and servile by making themselves objects of French colonial power. The grinding underdevelopment and discrimination against Arabs in the colonies therefore conspired with the cultural assault on the Arabs to spawn the waves of Arab migration to the colonial "mother country." Successive generations born in France now face the very same questioning of their fitness to be French and practitioners of French culture even though they are born in France, citizens of France, with no roots in an Arab heartland, just memories born out of travel, social media and contact. These successive generations are now the true Diaspora showing all the signs of separation from a mythic homeland whilst being castaways in the land of their birth. A tearing, violent state of alienation that invites all-encompassing extremist solutions that are hinged on binary dualities of black and white, devoid of shades of grey. This condition is the product of the power relations of the discourse of the Arab in France and its extremist expression in the instruments of biopower physically and spatially expressed as the banlieues.

Fanon ends his analysis of the condition of the Arab in France by utilising the concept of expatriation where he states as follows: "1. The North African will never be happier in Europe than at home, for he is asked to live without the very substance of his affectivity. 2. There is something manifestly and abjectly disingenuous in the above statement." (Fanon 1969 pg. 15). There is then a fundamental contradiction within Fanon's first statement of expatriation, for it is made without reference and due consideration of the colonial social order and its power relations that push the Arab to expatriate themselves from their native land to France. The fact that in France the Arab is faced with an assault on their affectivity, which indicates all that is human is under assault raises the issue of why then leave your native land for hostile, unwelcoming France. Fanon states: "If the standard of living made available to the North African in France is higher than the one he was accustomed to at home, this means that there is a good deal to be done in his country, in that 'other part of France.'" (Fanon 1969 pg. 15). Fanon after including the reality of the power relation between colonial metropole and colony now posits that the underdevelopment of the North African colonies is pushing the Arabs to France with its promise of a higher standard of living. Fanon sums up the reality of both France and the colonies for the Arab as follows: "It means that over the whole territory of the French nation (the metropolis and the French nation), there are tears to be wiped away, inhuman attitudes to be fought, condescending ways of speech to be ruled out, men to be humanised." (Fanon 1969 pg. 16). Under French colonial domination there is then no safe, affirmative space for the Arab both within his native land under French colonial domination and much less in France where the discourse of hegemonic white supremacy and its instruments of power relentlessly assault the Arab. In this scenario Arab expatriation is joined at the hips with repatriation but what is the present existential reality of those generations born in France? Repatriation is illegal but expatriation from France is real, simply a social reality that conjures up visions of the Final Solution now applied to Arabs in Europe. Fanon ends the article raising questions as to the heart of the matter and the finality of the Final Solution as follows: "If YOU do not reclaim the man who is before you, how can I assume that you reclaim the man that is in you? If YOU do not want the man who is before you, how can I believe the man that is perhaps in you? If YOU do not demand the man, if YOU do not sacrifice the man that is in you so that the man who is on this earth shall be more than a body, more than a Mohammed, by what conjurer's trick will I have to acquire the certainty that you, too, are worthy of my love." (Fanon 1969 pg. 16). Fanon presents the duality of the Arab and the white man where the dynamic for change or retrogression to the Final Solution is posed. The power relation Fanon describes is one in which the white man is dominant, even hegemonic, ensuring that the dynamic for change can only engage with specific action on the part of the white man. The white man has to reclaim the Arab, want the Arab, sacrifice the white man and demand a new man. Can all of us be convinced that the white man is a man imbued with humanity capable of being an agent of change? Failure to indicate these vitally necessary characteristics to change, then our primary conclusion is that the white man is only capable of actively pursuing the terminal state of his discourse and worldview, which is the Final Solution. A strategic terrain where our love or hate of the white man is irrelevant and of no consequence, for to choose love or hate in such a terrain potently illustrates

our weakness and the fact that we remain dominated in the 21st century in spite of the end of colonial domination but not neo-colonial domination. Fanon presents in encapsulated form the power relations of the binary duality of white /Arab with the whites wielding dominant, hegemonic power where a change in the power dynamic is hinged on the willingness and aptitude of the whites to forego domination in a bid to discover their humanity long immersed by the hegemonic discourse of white supremacy. In the second decade of the twenty-first century as in the decade of the 1950s of the twentieth century when Fanon published this article, the signs are not indicative of a change in the dynamics of the power relations of white/Arab, in fact they have grown more intractable and welcoming of the Final Solution as beneath the mask of the mass migration of Arabs who are Muslims to Europe, the fundamental question is the solution for the generations of Arabs born in France and Europe, the product of the Arab migration Fanon referred to in the 1950s. The buzz word that points to the concern with these generations of Arab citizens is integration and its use to justify programs/pogroms of the State to criminalise cultural practises deemed un-European/not white enough (NWE). This is just the thin edge of the wedge that leads to the culmination point, the Final Solution, as already there are a series of mini Kristallnacht events across Europe on Arabs, Roma, Africans and the Jews, as they intensify in numbers committed and persons attacked. Gestures pointing to the solution desired but failingly masked by a fraying camouflage of liberal lies, deceit and smiling faces.

Chapter 11
A Case of Black on Black Racism

In the article "West Indians and Africans" published in "Toward the African Revolution", which Fanon published in French in 1955, Fanon presents an analysis of black on black racism that is absent from "Black Skin White Masks", hence its strategic importance to this deconstruction of the discourse of Fanon presented in "Black Skin White Masks." In the article Fanon indicates that the book "Black Skin White Masks" dealt with "the problem of the coloured man in the white world." (Fanon 1969 pg. 17). Fanon in the article then posits that there is a reality that impacts relations of "Negro people" as follows: "I was not unaware of the fact that within the entity of the "Negro people" movements could be discerned which, unfortunately, were devoid of any attractive features. I mean, for example, that the enemy of the Negro is often not the white man but a man of his own colour. This is why I suggested the possibility of a study which could contribute to the dissolution of the affective complexes that could oppose West Indians and Africans." (Fanon 1969 pg. 17). Fanon wrote of the coloured man in the white world whilst being aware of the divisions, the lack of solidarity, the unattractive features of black on black relations. Fanon focuses on the affective complexes of black people where West Indians of African descent are in such a relation with Africans amounting to black on black racism as they are enemies facing off with each other to the benefit of the hegemonic white order. Fanon is then insisting that the affective complexes that plague black personalities under white hegemony divide and present such black persons as enemies of each other, thereby seeking to deflect the power relation between hegemonic whites and dominated blacks.

Negro People

For Fanon there is no Negro people as there is no homogeneous Negro race for this is a hollow concept propagandised by the Negro-baiters, the discursive agents of hegemonic white supremacist discourse. There is then a strategic purpose driving the acceptance of this concept of the Negro people necessary to domination of black people by white supremacist discourse. Fanon states:

"we should like to point out that his business of Negroes is a dirty business. A business which, when you are faced with it, leaves you wholly disarmed if you accept the premises of the Negro-baiters." (Fanon 1969 pg. 17). The Negro business is an instrument of power of white supremacist discourse dispersed by the Negro-baiters whose role it is to seduce the Negroes to accept Negro business as their business, as being their definition, identity and calling. In so doing, the accepting Negroes become disarmed, fit to be normalised, to turn themselves into objects/subjects of white hegemonic power, to be the ideal Negro aggregated into the Negro race. The product of Negro business is then the ideal, servile white Negro and the white Negro race, all the products of white hegemony.

Fanon continues on the reality of the "Negro people" as follows: "And when I say that the expression "Negro people" is an entity, I thereby indicate that, except for cultural influences, nothing is left. There is as a great difference between a West Indian and a Dakarian as between a Brazilian and a Spaniard. The object of lumping all Negroes together under the designation of 'Negro people' is to deprive them of any possibility of individual expression. What is thus attempted is to put them under the obligation of matching the idea one has of them." (Fanon 1969 pg. 17). Negro people is then for Fanon a fabrication devised by the Negro-baiters for a strategic purpose as it insists that there is a homogeneous entity when differences exist, are not recognised and acted upon. For Fanon the strategic intent is to erase and prohibit the development and expression of individuality. It is then an assault on black individuality, that drives a counter effort that overdetermines individuality to the detriment of the development and application of the solidarity necessary for resistance against white hegemony. The white race is then a mythic strategic construct necessary to the assault on non-white races towards sustainable white hegemony, but to conjure up the materiality, the specificity of the white race there must be Negro people, the Negro race. It is then the duty of the Negro-baiters through the ages to convince Negroes that there is a white race and you are part of the Negro people, race. This mythic strategic construct is the grand homogeneous agglomeration of the problem, of the threat that enables a multifaceted assault. Without this device, this mythic construct this, Negro people, the entire strategic assault flounders as it beguiles and seduces the object to accept and act upon the fear of the white homogeneous race and to wage war on the black homogeneous race that is defined by the black soul, that is the gift of the white race. But both races don't exist, they are constituted by white supremacist discourse and must then be constantly policed and normalised. They exist only in the minds and worldview of those who accept and make themselves an object of this white supremacist discourse. Hence Fanon's position that the unleashing of Negro people is a device to have Negroes seduced to execute the task of patterning themselves according to the model of the Negro as defined by white discourse. This is why Fanon stresses the difference between the West Indian and the African from Dakar as he does for white people, for homogeneity is a myth and the hollowness of the concept of the Negro people is apparent. The white and Negro races are then operationalised concepts that drive action in a social order only driven by race hate, racism is the actual driving force of both concepts. Both concepts are applied to conjure up the operational action terrain necessary for the social potency of racism/race hate. To assault race hate/racism both mythic concepts with its links to North Atlantic historico-political discourse must be dismantled.

Fanon continues in his assault on the discourse of the white race as follows: "Is it not obvious that there can only be a white race? What would the 'white people' correspond to? Do I have to explain the difference that exists between nation, people, fatherland, community? When one says 'Negro people' one systematically assumes that all Negroes agree on certain things, that they share a principle of community. The truth is that there is nothing, *a priori*, to warrant the assumption that such a thing as the Negro people exists. That there is an African people, that there is a West Indian people, this I do believe. 2 But when someone talks to me about that 'Negro people,' I try to understand what is meant. Then, unfortunately, I understand that there is in this a source of conflicts. Then I try to destroy this source." (Fanon 1969 pgs. 17-18). The discourse of white supremacy insists that only white folks constitute a race whilst Negroes can only be a people, a community. Fanon insists that there is no Negro community, people, fatherland and race, these are just mythic white constructs, but there are African people and West Indian people. For Fanon there are inherent conflicts embedded in the concept of the Negro people making it a source of conflict that must be assaulted and destroyed. Within this quotation Fanon attaches a footnote (2) which states as follows: "Let us say that the concessions we have made are fictitious. Philosophically and politically there is no such thing as an African people. There is an African world. And a West Indian world as well. On the other hand, it can be said there is a Jewish people; but not a Jewish race." (Fanon 1969 pg. 18). In the footnote Fanon debunks his position in the text that there are African and West Indian peoples as Fanon insists that he made fictitious concessions as philosophically, and philosophically there are only African and West Indian worlds. The only path to evolving a race, a people, a community with a fatherland becomes possible only when white racist hegemony is displaced and destroyed over the African and West Indian. For Fanon there is a Jewish people but no Jewish race.

Fanon now describes the research agenda of his article as follows: "What is at issue here? I say that in a period of fifteen years a revolution has occurred in West Indian-African relations. I want to show wherein this event consists." (Fanon 1969 pg. 18). Fanon is positing that in the space of fifteen years the black to black relations of West Indians and Africans have undergone a revolution. The onus is then on Fanon to prove his position of revolutionary change impacting this black to black relation. Fanon then deals with race in Martinique which is necessary to presenting his case. Fanon states: "The racial problem is covered over by economic discrimination and, in a given social class, it is above all productive of anecdotes. Relations are not modified by epidermal accentuations." "Here we have proof that questions of race are but a superstructure, a mantle, an obscure ideological emanation concerning an economic reality." (Fanon 1969 pg. 18). In Martinique race serves as the superstructure of an economic reality where the visible white minority dominates the economic order in the twentieth century, whilst blacks dominate the political order and other social spaces. White power has grave need of a discourse that assaults the view of the black self and their worldview to accept white domination of especially the economic order. The issue is not then epidermal accentuation as in the North Atlantic as this is not a strategically important instrument of power in 20th century Martinique. What is crucially important is acceptance of and acting on the view that white dominance of the economic order is the necessary path to Martinican development. What is now strategically necessary is acceptance and action to preserve and expand white economic hegemony over a black majority population. The race discourse is then formulated to divide the black majority and win acceptance of the need for, and action to preserve and expand exclusive white spaces for they are better endowed to be successful at what they do in the economic order than black people. Race is then a superstructure driven by a racist white hegemonist discourse that is relentlessly striving to seduce the black politicians to ensure the sustainability of this white hegemony, for the black politicians will in turn handle the black masses.

In ending this section of his article Fanon now focuses on the role of irony in the West Indies and the need to appreciate this role in order to understand the utilisation of language and its meanings. Fanon states: "One must be accustomed to what is called the spirit of Martinique in order to grasp the meaning of what is said." "It is true that in the West Indies irony is a mechanism of defence against neurosis. A West Indian, in particular an intellectual who is no longer on the level of irony, discovers his Negritude. Thus, while in Europe irony protects against the existential anguish, in Martinique it protects against the awareness of Negritude." (Fanon 1969 pg. 19). The spirit of Martinique and the West Indies is the use of irony in communication and in worldview to self-medicate in response to the neuroses that afflict those assaulted by the discourse of white supremacy. Fanon insists that emancipation from the need for self-medication only ends with the embrace of Negritude, but in Martinique irony stands in the way of the embrace of Negritude and ultimately the hegemony of Negritude over the discourses of the social order. In the West Indies the assault of neuroses drives the adoption of irony in an attempt to mask the assault of these neuroses, to camouflage the human under assault and to evade the assault. This tactic and the instrument utilised blocks the embrace of Negritude as Negritude demands confrontation with the white supremacist discourse mounting the attack whilst, irony seeks only to mitigate an assault as it cannot end the assault. Irony is then an instrument of power of white supremacist discourse that constitutes an entire culture of irony which is essentially a shucking and jiving culture incapable of liberation, as it insists that the price to be paid for change is too high, eat little and live long and half a bread is better than none! It plays at criticism as it simulates a process of questioning and complaining whilst deeply appreciative of the status quo.

That is the sublime irony - questioning without intent to struggle which is in fact fatalistic resignation with a veneer of questioning. Shucking and jiving in the 21st century. In Europe Fanon insists that the black minority utilises irony to self-medicate the sickness arising from the pain of existence in Europe, but with a different operational terrain to that of the West Indies, for irony has to soothe your ever present ache caused by the fear of being the visible, despised minority in a continent with the undeniable penchant for the Final Solution. In ending this section Fanon states: "It can be seen that a study of irony in the West Indies is crucial for the sociology of this region. Aggressiveness there is almost always cushioned by irony." (Fanon 1969 pg. 19). This is so given the problematic of being non-white where your ontology is in fact problematic at best, as it is defined for you by hegemonic racist discourse which problematizes you to the point where your aggressive action is expressed via irony by you, by the victim and by the social order. For aggression problematizes the action, the victim and the social order hence the irony of it all. This is especially apparent in the gun violence of the West Indies of the 21st century and the manner in which perpetrator, victim, politicians, media and social media interpret and express the meanings attached to these acts of gun violence. Shucking and jiving driven by irony in a quest for relief that is never forthcoming.

Fanon divides his analysis into the pre-Second World War period and the post-Second World War period.

Before the Second World War

Fanon describes the West Indian concept of the African before the Second World war as follows: "at every level of West Indian society an inescapable feeling of superiority develops, becomes systematic, hardens. In every West Indian before 1939, there was not only the certainty of superiority over the African, but the certainty of a fundamental difference. The African was a Negro and the West Indian a European." (Fanon 1969 pg. 20). Enslavement and colonisation has resulted in the Negro West Indian conceiving of being superior to the African as he was inherently different from the African for he was European and not Negro for only Africans are Negroes and since he was not African he must be European. The West Indian was then deeply afflicted with hallucinatory whiteness. Fanon continues: "The result to which we wish to draw attention is that, whatever the field considered, the West Indian was superior to the African, of a different species, assimilated to the metropolitan. But as inasmuch as externally the West Indian was just a little bit African, since, say what you will, he was black, he was obliged-as a normal reaction in psychological economy-to harden his frontiers in order to be protected against any misapprehension." (Fanon 1969 pg. 20). The West Indian beguiled and besieged by hallucinatory whiteness is forever on the defensive expecting and awaiting the opportunity to debunk the misapprehension that grates at his being when his blackness is mistaken for him being African. The West Indian is then condemned to perpetually expect and to assault the mistaken identity and to defend his "true" identity of being European. The West Indian is then relentlessly assaulting his black self, thereby turning himself into an object of white power, normalising and policing himself to ensure sustainable hegemonic white power. Fanon continues on the West Indian hatred for the African as follows: "We may say that the West Indian, not satisfied to be superior to the African, despised him, and while the white man could allow himself certain liberties with the native, the West Indian could not. This was because, between whites and Africans, there was no need of a reminder: the differences stared one in the face. But what a catastrophe if the West Indian should suddenly be taken for an African." (Fanon 1969 pg. 20). The West Indian despised the African because both are assaulted by the same discourse of epidermalisation throwing the West Indian superiority complex into disarray and crisis unlike the white man who was exonerated from this assault of epidermalisation. This then allowed the perfection of the black on black racism that divided asunder the African and the West Indian whilst allowing the white man to play both sides of the black divide as their benefactor, protector from the black enemy and their desirable role model. In other words, the living embodiment of all that is civilised and inherently superior hence living expressions of the only lifestyle worthy of emulation. Black on black racism is then the most potent expression of the assault of the discourse of white supremacy on black people. Fanon states on this as follows: "We may say also that this position of the West Indian was authenticated by the European. The West Indian was not a Negro; he was a West Indian, that is to say a quasi-metropolitan. By this attitude the white man justified the West Indian in his contempt for the African. The

Negro, in short, was a man who inhabited Africa." (Fanon 1969 pg. 20). The white man gave impetus to the position and agenda of the West Indian vis-a-vis the African as it divided the race and placed the white man in the position of broker of definition and respectability to both. The West Indian then formulated the completely untenable self-conceptualisation of being quasi-white, honorary white, quasi-metropolitan, a convoluted state of non-being that was possible only in the West Indies where the power relations gave it purpose, definition and specificity. Transported to Europe with this conception of self the West Indian was in for a rude awakening. To protect this untenable state of non-being the West Indian then invented the dichotomy of space in a desperate bid to redefine the white man's discourse of the epidermalisation of the black by insisting that there are only Negroes in Africa not in the West Indies, which survives to this day. Fanon continues on this theme as follows: "The African, for his part, was in Africa the real representative of the Negro race." "The West Indian was a black man, but the Negro was in Africa." "But it can be affirmed that in the West Indies in 1939 no spontaneous claim of Negritude rang forth." (Fanon 1969 pg. 21). In 1939 in the French West Indies the discourse of black on black racism attained the desired strategic effect as there was no embrace of, no recognition of the need for black centred consciousness arising from the womb of popular culture, of mass black consciousness. The West Indian black was then comfortable in her/his hallucinatory whiteness and its discourse of self-immolation and black on black racism with its attendant worldview and instruments of power and normalisation. Fanon will next in the article present the events that impacted West Indian hallucinatory whiteness precipitating a crisis of servile identity which gave space to the emergence of the discourse of Negritude and its impact on the social order. The crisis of West Indian hallucinatory whiteness was in fact spawned by the impact of the Second World war on France and the West Indies.

The Second World war

The Nazi conquest and occupation of France dealt a grave blow to the fatherland of the West Indian plagued with hallucinatory whiteness. Fanon states as follows on this blow: "The downfall of France, for the West Indian was in a sense the murder of the father." (Fanon 1969 pg. 22). The Nazi conquest and the subsequent colonial occupation of the fatherland for the first time spanning the era of French colonial conquest in the West Indies to the twentieth century, the black afflicted with hallucinatory whiteness experienced the eclipse of all that they longed for and hoped to emulate ruthlessly conquered and colonised by adherents of a discourse that insisted on the extermination of the black race. At this point in the West Indies alienation was now married to anomie. The second grave blow the second world war and the conquest and colonial occupation of France delivered to those afflicted with hallucinatory whiteness was the exile of vessels and their crews of the French fleet in the French West Indies for the duration of the occupation of France during the second world war. This unleashed some 10,000 white, racist, armed French military personnel on Martinique who were enabled by the war time powers to actively seek to exert hegemony over the black majority of the social order. These 10,000 armed, white racists and their families simply threatened the sustainability of the social order created before the war. Their dependence on the local economy deeply throttled the local economy and their racist assaults on the black majority revived the memories of massa on the plantation, further deepening the anomie of those suffering under the loss of their fatherland. Fanon insists that this existential reality constituted the first metaphysical experience as follows: "The Martiniquan held those white racists responsible for all this. The West Indian, in the presence of those men who despised him, began to have misgivings as to his values. The West Indian went through his first metaphysical experience." (Fanon 1969 pg. 23). This first metaphysical experience was then anomie as the black West Indian in the face of the reality of the impacts of the second world war on the social order and their individual lives were now forced into a defensive order, a situation where resistance was on the agenda to be considered as a valid response. There were then choices available as there always are with power: to surrender and embrace your anomic existential reality or to search for paths leading to liberation out of anomie. Fanon posits that the condition of anomie was forced into resistance by the operationalisation of two discourses in the French West Indies at the time: the discourse of Negritude of Aime Cesaire which predated the war with little traction and the discourse of Free France by De Gaulle. The discourse of Free France totally discredited the colonial regime of the French West Indies and its armed, racist military personnel by insisting that they were collaborators with the Nazi conqueror of France being the fifth columnists that enabled the conquest of France. Black West Indians saw hope for the resurgence of their fatherland and the return to "normalcy" but the question of resistance to the collaborators dominating the West Indies placed the issue of countering the white racists firmly on the agenda. This resistance in aid of recovering the fatherland then demanded an instrument to blunt the racist assault of the white, racist collaborators. Black resistance to recover the fatherland was now demanding the resurgence of and the utilisation of black consciousness/Negritude which meant that Cesaire's discourse framed the question and then answered it by positioning Negritude as the weapon of assault. Fanon states: "But the consequences that concerns us is the following: before ten thousand racists, the West Indian felt obliged to defend himself. Without Cesaire this would have been difficult for him." For two years the West Indian defended the 'virtuous colour' inch by inch and, without expecting it, was dancing on the edge of a precipice. For after all, if the colour black is virtuous, I shall be all the more virtuous the blacker I am." (Fanon 1969 pg.23). The West Indian was now dancing on the edge of a precipice as they were now using Cesaire's discourse of Negritude to recover, regenerate and restore their white fatherland and the social order premised on white hegemony they were active in before the impact of the second world war. But Cesaire's Negritude was the incendiary instrument utilised to attain this strategic end of the resurgence of the past, but the instrument in its impact on human perception, unleashed visions of a world and a social order directly in contradiction with the strategy of fatherland resurgence. This variance between discourse, instrument and end sought resulted in tensions within the resistance movement that demanded resolution. As to the nature of this precipice Fanon states: "This amounted to nothing less than requiring the West Indian totally to recast his world, to undergo a metamorphosis of his body. It meant demanding of him an axiological activity in reverse, a valorisation of what he had rejected. (Fanon 1969 pg. 24). The black West Indian with the adoption of the discourse of Aime Cesaire as the instrument of resistance to the hegemony of the French collaborators with Nazi Germany generated a crisis of being of the black west Indian as she/he was now under pressure to reshape their world, to fabricate a new world where the black and blackness were the defining centrality, the new locus of power. The West Indian was now forced to embrace and have this rejected discourse impact his affixed black soul whereby the black West Indian was applying a discourse of liberation willingly to her/his being in the quest for the past. The rejected was now afforded value where it had none before and this constituted an axiological reverse as blackness and blacks were now afforded value never afforded before. The instruments of power of hegemonic white supremacist discourse were now under assault in the French West Indies especially in Martinique.

The invasion and liberation of France by the Allies in 1943 constituted a crisis in Martinique as the collaborators and their armed racist military were still exerting hegemony over Martinique creating the need to liberate Martinique from the collaborators but then what? The strategic action chosen was public mass demonstrations during the months of July and August 1943 indicating their rejection of the collaborators of the period of Nazi occupation and the call for a new regime. But with the removal of the collaborators is it the hope to return to business as usual exemplified by the social order of the pre-war years? Fanon states: "Martinique for the first time systematised its political consciousness. In Martinique, the first metaphysical, or if one prefers, ontological experiment, coincides with the first political experiment. The proletariat of Martinique is a systematised Negro." (Fanon 1969 pg. 24). Fanon insists that the liberation movement of Martinique gave birth to a politically and ontologically conscious proletariat. The ontological dynamic triggered by the drive for liberation, defined by Cesaire's Negritude, was then combined with the political consciousness driven by the liberation movement resulting in the birth of the systematised Negro. The combination of a socialist political worldview with Negritude is then the basis of the systematised Negro of Martinique but is there in this systematisation a desire for liberation from France and the will to undertake the process of permanent revolution? More importantly what is the nature of the discourse that drives the systematisation of the Negro in Martinique for therein lies the potency of hegemonic discourse to penetrate and subvert the resistance through the opportunity and space afforded by systematisation utilising discourses of the enlightenment as socialism/communism. A systematised Negro is not then posing a certain threat to white hegemonic discourse for you can be systematised in the service of the hegemony of white supremacist discourse. The fact that today Martinique is an overseas territory of France speaks for itself illustrating the reality that white supremacist discourse will not surrender and walk away.

After the war

In this period Fanon points to the core changes in the West Indian worldview that arose in the process of liberation as follows: "Thus the West Indian, after 1945, changed his values. Whereas before 1945 he had his eyes riveted on white Europe, whereas what seemed good to him was escape from his colour, in 1945 he discovered himself to be not only black but a Negro, and it was in the direction of distant Africa that he was henceforth to put out his feelers." (Fanon 1969 pgs. 24-25). Both the West Indian and the Negro in France now accepted their black selves and turned to Africa in their quest for wholeness. Fanon continues: "They came to Africa with their hearts full of hope, eager to rediscover the source, to suckle at the authentic breasts of the African earth. After 1945 they changed their tune. They said to the Africans, 'Don't pay attention to my white skin, my soul is black as yours, and that is what matters.'" (Fanon 1969 pg. 25). At the point of the post 1945 return to blackness and accompanying longing for Africa, Fanon is insisting that the West Indian was in a condition uncertainty, of in-betweenity, of being neither black nor white, hence the fixation with Africa for the second world war had in fact traumatised the product of white supremacist discourse. Fanon next states that the African rejected the West Indian's quest for definition as follows: "During this time the African pursued his way. He was not torn; he did not have to situate himself simultaneously with reference to the West Indian and with reference to the European. These last belonged in the same bag, the bag of the starvers, of the exploiters, of the no-goods." "They rejected the West Indian, reminding him that *they* had not deserted, that *they* had not betrayed, that *they* had toiled, suffered, struggled on the African earth. The West Indian had said no to the white man; the African was saying no to the West Indian." (Fanon 1969 pgs. 25-26). The African rooted in their African culture had no similar impact from the second world war, in fact the war enabled the African space to visualise and set in train the strategy of decolonisation, unlike that of the West Indies. The African had no psychic nor strategic need to situate herself/

himself simultaneously with the white man and the West Indian. The African then dismissed the West Indian as the lackey, the vassal of the white coloniser sharing the space from which grave threats are posed to Africans with the white man. The African then after 1945 openly rejected the West Indian. Fanon states: "The latter was undergoing his second metaphysical experience. He then suffered despair. Haunted by impurity, overwhelmed by sin, riddled with guilt, he was prey to the tragedy of being neither white nor Negro." "The African was getting his revenge and the West Indian was paying." (Fanon 1969 pgs. 25-26). The West Indian was on the quest for wholeness in Africa, convinced that an immersion in their concept of Africa will heal all their infirmities for the West Indian was condemned to a state of in-betweenity, of an indeterminate state of being neither hither nor thither. Neither white or black. In such an indeterminate state of existence, driven by a quest for wholeness, the West Indian posed the grave threat of seeking to redefine Africa in their image and likeness, to the detriment of the African as the potential to aid and abet the white colonial enterprise in pursuit of this West Indian quest was plausible and real. In pursuit of the West Indian quest, West Indians had the propensity to constitute a West Indian soul of Africa through the West Indian discourse of Africa. The danger then is Diasporic discourses of Africa cobbled together in the west under the hegemony of white supremacist discourse in pursuit of the quest for wholeness. This plausible threat posed from the Diaspora is expressed in Fanon's analysis of the social order of Martinique with specific reference to the Black West Indian and the white man as follows: "we may say that in Martinique, before 1939, there was not one side the Negro and on the other side the white man, but a scale of colours the intervals of which could readily be passed over. One needed to have children by someone less black than oneself. There was no racial barrier, no discrimination. There was that ironic spice, so characteristic of the Martinique mentality. But in Africa the discrimination was real. There the Negro, the African, the native, the black, the dirty, was rejected, despised, cursed. There an amputation had occurred; there humanity was denied." (Fanon 1969 pg. 26). The nature of white hegemony in Martinique was vastly different to that of Africa, where in Martinique the minority whites pursued an entirely different strategy from that of the minority whites pursued in Africa. In Martinique the strategy was assimilation, to constitute a black West Indian who was white and entirely supportive of the social order. The African strategy was premised on hard core policed white supremacist domination in keeping with the West Indian slave plantation which refused to embrace the strategy of assimilation. The threat that arises from Martinique is then black West Indians in search of wholeness in Africa intent on defining Africa in keeping with the Martiniquan strategy, intent on creating a soul for Africans which will enable their transformation into assimilated Africans intent on replicating the Martinican model in Africa driven by a West Indian discourse of Africa. This discourse of Africa retains at its core the white supremacist discursive constructs as those of the enlightenment that inevitably move to replicate sustainable white supremacist hegemony in Africa. The post war political reality of Africa potently illustrates the potency of the white supremacist model utilised in colonial Africa, with the number of African politicians acting on their servility to the white overlords of the North Atlantic far outnumbering those African political leaders who refused to be servile and paid the ultimate price for this independence. Fanon in his final work "The Wretched of the Earth" succinctly dealt with this African reality. In this article Fanon's idyllic depiction of Martinique versus Africa expresses the vast difference between two models of white domination which both constitute servile non-whites that actively work towards white supremacist hegemony. But in the 21st century Martinique, Guadeloupe and French Guiana are all overseas departments of France whilst in continental Africa there are no such overseas departments which illustrates the potency of the discursive structures unleashed in the West Indies from the slave plantation to the overseas department. It must be noted that in 1946 Martinique, Guadeloupe and French Guiana became overseas departments which was in effect the political response to the quest for liberation, especially in Martinique, and it has had its desired strategic effect. Fanon ends the article with a potent statement that questions his idyllic statements made previously in the article as follows: "It thus seems that the West Indian, after the great white error, is now living in the great black mirage." (Fanon 1969 pg. 27). First for the West Indian there is hallucinatory whiteness where she/he is white, specifically European, which is the great error of delusion by accepting as possible and valid the ability of black people to become white. The rejection of the great white error now leads the West Indian to the great black mirage where she/he is standing in awe and wonder staring at an optical illusion of blackness and liberation. But staring in wonder and awe at blackness and liberation is simply not good enough, not adequate to the task of liberation, for this task requires personal action, mass action and political action underpinned by a discourse of liberation. The black mirage is then the West Indian staring in wonder and awe at a black mirage accepting the optical illusion of liberation of the mirage as being real. Therefore, seduced into talking black liberation but refusing to act to attain black liberation potently illustrated by the politics of the overseas department of Martinique for the black mirage insists that you are already doing what is required for we are liberated, all in our head, not in the reality of the power relations.

In 1946 white supremacist discourse went on the offensive to recover its hegemony in Martinique by now proclaiming that the fatherland is no longer in Europe but right here, in the French overseas departments of the Caribbean basin. The fatherland is now made manifest on Caribbean soil potently indicating that the pre 1939 order is now, has the means and the opportunity to become even more evolved as assimilation will now take place in and via the expression of the fatherland in the Caribbean. A strategy only France among the colonial powers present in the Caribbean dared to implement, such was the nature of the threat to hegemony visualised from the events of 1945 in Martinique. The political strategy unleashed in 1946 attained its strategic end potently illustrated by the politics of Martinique in the 21st century, especially the issues of identity and independence and a social order that is a 21st century post-overseas department evolution of the pre-1939 social order. From 1946 to the present the hegemonic instrument of power in this context is black on black racism working to ensure the hegemony of white supremacist discourse, indicating the reality that liberation remains elusive.

Chapter 12
Racism as an Instrument of Power

In September 1956 in Paris Fanon delivered his speech to the First Congress of Negro Writers and Artists which was published in French in 1956. This speech was translated into English and published in "Toward The African Revolution" titled "Racism and Culture" and is deconstructed in the text that follows.

Normative values and its Paradox

This text of Fanon is included in this study as it is one of his most potent statements on the nature of power and racism in the North Atlantic in the four texts published in the 1950s and 1960s before and after his death. In this text Fanon states at its beginning as follows: "The unilaterally decreed normative value of certain cultures deserves our careful attention. One of the paradoxes immediately encountered is the rebound of egocentric, sociocentric definitions. There is first assumed the existence of human groups having no culture; then of a hierarchy of cultures; and finally, the concept of cultural relativity. We have here the whole range from overall negation to singular and specific recognition." (Fanon 1969 pg. 31). The imperial insistence that there are specific cultures that possess and exhibit specific, unique normative values that create a hierarchy of cultures is then the basis of the imperial power relation where racism serves as an instrument of imperialist power. That certain specific cultures possess and exhibit these normative values and others do not then mean that normative values are the basis of difference, the expression of superiority and the normalising instrument of power both in the culture where these values are naturally occurring in its culture and in other cultures devoid of these values. In these inferior cultures the normative values are applied to police this culture and to convince the adherents of this inferior, underdeveloped culture to become objects of power that these normative values serve. Without these normative values there would be no North Atlantic hegemony over the world hence these values constitute manifest destiny. Fanon points to the egocentric and sociocentric definitions which flow with the discourse of white exceptionalism where egocentrism and sociocentrism of the white man merge to constitute the discourse of white supremacy. The white man is the product of his unique normative values rooted in a specific and unique social order driven by these said normative values most eloquently summed up by Max Weber in his racist work "The Protestant Ethic and the Spirit of Capitalism." The discourse of normative values is first seeking to mask the power relations of the white man's social order and justify his imperial enterprise, but white racism as an instrument of power exposes the reality behind the mask. For normalisation is a mechanism of power in the white man's social order, with racism being an instrument of power, which means that racism in the white world cannot be for itself and by itself, it can only be an instrument of power. Racism is then one tool power in the North Atlantic utilises to normalise a social order, and by which to dominate an inferior race situated in a social order in the periphery and in the metropole.

The Enterprise of Deculturation

Fanon continues: "There are, we may say, certain constellations of institutions, established by particular men, in the framework of precise geographical areas, which at a given moment have undergone a direct and sudden assault of different cultural patterns. The technical, generally advanced development of the social group that has thus appeared enabled it to set up an organised domination. The enterprise of deculturation turns out to be the negative of a more gigantic work of economic, and even biological enslavement." (Fanon 1969 pg. 31). Fanon insists that there is an enterprise of deculturation which serves the power relation of economic and biological enslavement, where cultures are assaulted with deculturation in the quest to dominate these cultures towards attaining the strategic end of creating an order of enslavement that enables sustainable economic exploitation, both colonial and neo colonial, buttressed by the servility of those exploited attained through biological enslavement. The power relations of the sustainable economic order desired, demands the utilisation of racism as a normative instrument of power and there can be no racism as a normative instrument of power in the absence of biological enslavement. The entire process of domination sought and attained commences and is rendered sustainable with cultural assault and deculturation, of which racism is a strategic necessity, which means that racism resides in the bowels of capitalist mechanisms of power and it drives the capitalist North Atlantic state. Racism weaponises culture and frames the mechanism of deculturation in its assigned task to serve power and its quest for structures of exploitation by which wealth is generated, for wealth generation enables power to penetrate all spaces of the social order. The mistake lies in focusing and agonising on the cultural assault, the deculturation and the racism, whilst failing to visualise the overarching economic structure and the power relations that penetrate, that are diffused through and travel through them all, exercising power and tackling resistance. This reality destroys the applicability and relevance of attempts to use the same dominant formula supposedly in resistance in a quest for liberation.

Racism and Culture

In the text Fanon now deals with racism and culture as follows: "The doctrine of cultural hierarchy is but one aspect of systematised hierarchisation implacably pursued. The apparition of racism is not fundamentally determining. Racism is not the whole but the most visible, the more day-to-day and, not to mince matters, the crudest element of a given structure." "To study the relations of racism and culture is to raise the question of their reciprocal action." "it can be said that racism is indeed a cultural element. There are thus cultures with racism and cultures without racism." (Fanon 1969 pgs. 31-32). The discourse of cultural hierarchy is not a standalone entity, but a part of a hierarchy that is the expression of and rooted in an order that is hierarchalised with its hegemonic discourse and its attendant worldview which orders the world into a specific hierarchical order, where racism is but one instrument of power to attain and ensure the sustainability of this specific hierarchalised order. This specific order must then have an operational power structure that makes the order real and operational, of which racism is an intrinsic part. Racism is then very visible, but not the hegemonic determining agent of this order as it masks the nature of power and that of the hierarchical order, for whenever we insist that racism is the be all and end all of the white man and white culture we are then failing to recognise the potent nature of the threat posed. For Fanon we must follow the trail of racism to the operational structure that utilises it to then unearth and deconstruct the power relations that drive the structure, towards liberation. To do this we have then to recognise the reciprocal relationship between racism and culture, where racism is in fact a cultural element which then leads to the relationship between culture, hegemonic discourse and power. The quest can never begin and end with racism, for this is the methodology of continued docility, shucking and jiving and most of all, of being racist, a condition which ensures our enslavement to the hierarchical white order. Fanon continues on his analysis of racism as a cultural element as follows: "This precise cultural element, however, has not become encysted. Racism has not managed to harden. It has had to renew itself, to adapt itself, to change its appearance. It has had to undergo that fate of the cultural whole that informed it." (Fanon 1969 pg. 32). Racism as a cultural element is an instrument of power, hence it must remain dynamic, fluid and adaptable to strategically respond to power relations on a real time basis. Racism as culture does not have the luxury of becoming fixed by definition and meaning across time and space, for power demands of its mechanisms of power comprising the instruments of power pragmatism in application not dogmatism. Dogmatic, encysted and hardened racism is of no use to power and can present a grave threat to sustainable power exercised by specific groups within the social order in two ways: it presents a challenge to hegemonic power and discourse and secondly it renders power incapacitated to defeat the ongoing challenge of resistance that constantly arises from power/force relations. These impacts can lead to the loss of power by those groups that exercise hegemonic power at worst, or minimally social instability. Fanon continues: "This racism that aspires to be rational, individual, genotypically and phenotypically determined, becomes transformed into cultural racism. At the extreme, such terms as 'message' and 'cultural style' are resorted to. 'Occidental values' oddly blend with the already famous appeal of the 'cross against the crescent.'" (Fanon pgs. 32-33). The old, early twentieth century North Atlantic "scientific racism", taken to its extreme development by National Socialism, must now be compliant to the hegemony of post second world war cultural racism, where "scientific racism" and National Socialism are disposed of and replaced by a liberal, human rights centric cultural racism, where the message is masked, coded but remains potent even more potent than under the Nazi and "scientific racism" incarnations. Fanon notes that this cultural racism through its racist construct of "occidental values" has appropriated the very old racist construct of the "cross against the crescent", which under the hegemony of cultural racism moulds Islam and Arabs as grave threats. The terrain of the politics of Europe in the 21st century is then dominated by the battle for hegemony between the discourse of cultural racism and the adherents of a subordinate discourse of "scientific racism"/National Socialism which is presenting grave threats to the order of power. The possibility of this challenge for hegemony is relentlessly created by the commonality of the discourse of Islam and the Arab, that is common to both contending discourses, which can result in a pragmatic compromise between warring factions which will be rooted in dealing with the threat of the Arab and Islam in Europe, the common grave threats. In this scenario cultural racism will then bare its masked fangs and claws, generating allusions to the past from imperial colonial domination to the Fascists and National Socialists.

Colonial Oppression and the Oppressing People

Fanon in the text now deals with the nature of colonial oppression and the oppressing people as follows: "Racism, as we have seen, is only one element of a vaster whole: that of a systematised oppression of a people. How does an oppressing people behave? Here we rediscover constants. We witness the destruction of cultural values, of ways of life." "Such attempts deliberately leave out of account the special character of the colonial situation." "The enslavement, in the strictest sense, of the native population is the prime necessity." "The social panorama is destructured; values are flaunted, crushed, emptied. The lines of force, having crumbled, no longer give directions. In their stead a new system of values is imposed, not proposed but affirmed, by the heavy weight of cannons and sabres." (Fanon 1969 pgs. 33-34). Fanon rooted in his paradigm that racism is simply an instrument serving an overarching strategy of power is focusing on the nature of the oppressive people by citing the constants of oppression, namely the fact that the overarching strategy is only realisable with the enslavement of the native people. To attain this end, the assault of the oppressive people must be in the realm of culture, where racism is a vitally necessary tool of the assault. This cultural racist assault constitutes a special situation which demands a special explanation, but such explanations are not forthcoming and cannot be forthcoming from North Atlantic discourses. The line of assault is composite, combining a discursive assault at the cultural level and a military assault of the maxim guns and howitzers which destroys the line of force, the structure of power and the terrain of power relations in the targeted space, which spells anomie married to alienation, thereby opening the space to the culture of the oppressor to exert power towards hegemony. The oppressor then fills violently the void created by her/his assault which manifests itself in the destructuring of the native social order and culture which renders both the culture and social order decapitated and open to destruction which the oppressor nation desires, for this is what the strategy demands. On the strategy for the native culture of the oppressor Fanon states: "The setting up of the colonial system does not of itself bring about the death of the native culture. Historical observation reveals, on the contrary, that the aim sought is rather a continued agony than a total disappearance of the pre-existing culture. This culture once living and open to the future, becomes closed, fixed in the colonial status, caught in the yoke of oppression. Both present and mummified, it testifies against its members." (Fanon 1969 pg. 34). The assault of the oppressor on native culture is not to exterminate it and replace it with the culture of the oppressor, but to systematically destructure native culture rendering it a dual entity trapped in a specific time/space continuum, a colonial time/space continuum where the present is joined to a mummified culture which cannot respond in real time as it has no dynamic, no evolutionary acumen as its lines of force, its structure of power and the terrain of power relations are all now external of this culture and under the control of the oppressor. This duality of presence and death mediates the power relations of the oppressor with the oppressed, thereby incapacitating the ability of the oppressed to perceive and act against their oppression, hence the reason for its survival. The oppressor has then hollowed out the native culture by capturing its structure of power with its mechanisms of power and the terrain of power relations, thereby ensuring that the dynamic of the prevailing social order is under the hegemony of the oppressor. What are then left of the native culture are all the mummified vestiges of the native structure of power and the terrain of power relations which are under the hegemony of the oppressor utilised to seduce the native to become objects of oppressor power. This gutted native culture presents no plausible threat to the hegemony of the oppressor whilst it problematizes the native.

Cultural Mummification

For Fanon this gutted native culture impacts the native as follows: "this cultural mummification leads to a mummification of individual thinking. The apathy so universally noted among colonial peoples is but the logical consequence of this operation." "Thus we witness the setting up of archaic, inert institutions, functioning under the oppressor's supervision and patterned like a caricature of formerly fertile institutions." (Fanon 1969 pg. 34). A mummified culture constitutes individuals devoid of the ability to think dynamically, rather their perceptions are trapped in an ossified netherworld spawned by a culture gutted of its power, hence mummified. The oppressor then erects mummified institutions manned by mummified individuals to manage the affairs of the natives on a daily basis which further encapsulates native culture and daily pragmatic life in the netherworld of mummification and powerlessness, whilst confirming the white discourse of the colonised and the inferior races. With independence this mummified colonial legacy is eagerly embraced by the specially chosen natives the colonial state was handed over to for safe keeping. The mummified native state and the colonial state cannot function in the absence of the order of power of the oppressor hence the collapse, the violence and the power the North Atlantic continues to wield in these mummified countries of the periphery, in spite of independence! Fanon insists that the strategy of the oppressor is then to objectify the native culture, the native, the social order and the structure of power as follows: "Rather, this behaviour betrays a determination to objectify, to confine, to imprison, to harden. Phrases such as 'I know them,' 'that the way they are,' show this maximum objectification successfully achieved." "Exoticism is one of the forms of this simplification. It allows no cultural confrontation. As against this, we find characteristics, curiosities, things, never structure." "The social group, militarily and economically subjugated, is dehumanised in accordance with a polydimensional method." (Fanon 1969 pgs. 34-35). The assault on the native and the social order consists of a number of dimensions of assault operating simultaneously to attain the strategic end of a dehumanised, servile native existing in a servile, powerless social order. The intent then is to objectify, which confines and imprisons the native, whilst hardening the captivity of the native in the social order, which is a captive of the oppressors. This objectification which amounts to simplification, to exoticism where there is no structure to the native social order, hence there is no cultural confrontation between native culture and the culture of the oppressor. There can be no structure to native culture as it has been gutted of its structure of power and the terrain of power relations is no longer theirs but under the hegemony of the oppressor. What is instructive is the fact that the basis of black on black racism is the objectification, the simplification, the destructuring, the exoticism and the confinement of the black enemy in a quest for racist hegemony. Black on black racism is then the most potent expression of the condition of the native and the most potent instrument of the polydimensional method of assault towards assuring sustainable hegemony of the oppressor. For with black on black racism we turn the apathy of the conquered into action against those as ourselves, where we are bent on exhibiting our rage on those as ourselves, in search for release from our cowardice to confront the oppressor.

In the text Fanon returns to the analysis of racism as follows: "The perfecting of the means of production inevitably brings about the camouflage of the techniques by which man is exploited, hence of the forms of racism. It is therefore not as a result of the evolution of people's minds that racism loses its virulence. No inner revolution can explain this necessity for racism to seek more subtle forms, to evolve. On all sides men become free, putting an end to the lethargy to which oppression and racism had condemned them." (Fanon 1969 pgs.35-36). Fanon insists that racism evolves in response to the power relations of the day and the resulting change in the prime strategic end where racism takes on a liberal mask and tone with the evolution of the social order which Fanon pins to the development of the mode of production. Racism has then to change its discourse and its operational strategy expressed through its strategy to beguile and seduce its targets. This strategy demands effective masks as to its strategic intent which must be effectively camouflaged which prohibits the use of old school "scientific racism," Fascism and National Socialism, worse yet those throwbacks to colonial era racism. The reversion to these discarded forms of racism in the North Atlantic in the 21st century is then effectively challenging the potency of the globalised, neoliberal order of racism in the quest for the hegemony of an old, dysfunctional racist order that is of little use to the social order of the day rooted in globalised, neoliberal financial markets capitalism. Fanon is warning that the change in the nature of racism has nothing to do with a change in the worldview of the oppressor, for there is no revolution that grasps humanity, just a new strategy dictated by the evolving social order of the oppressor. Fanon then warns us on the grave impact racism has on the social order as follows: "The social constellation, the cultural whole, are deeply modified by the existence of racism." "We must tirelessly look for the repercussions of racism at all levels of sociability." (Fanon pg. 36). Racism impacts and modifies the social order, as it must do as an instrument of power, there are then power relations exercised through all spaces of the social order which express these impacts of racism on human consciousness, interactions and subsequently on what is deemed sociable. Fanon continues: "The truth is that the rigor of the system made the daily affirmation of a superiority superfluous." "The commercial undertaking of enslavement, of cultural destruction, progressively gave way to a verbal mystification." (Fanon 1969 pg. 37). The project of enslavement and cultural destruction evolves to the point where there is no longer the need for the daily insistence of the superiority of the oppressor and the instruments of violence to enforce this affirmed superiority, for the effectiveness of the assault renders these instruments irrelevant. At this point, the oppressed are sustainably making themselves objects of power, power relations supplant those of graphic violence and verbal mystification rooted in hegemonic discourse is the preferred instrument of power. In this operational environment the discourse and methodology of racism evolves into the liberal order of North Atlantic racism. On racism Fanon continues as follows: "Racism bloats and disfigures the face of the culture that practices it." "This means that a social group, a country, a civilisation, cannot be unconsciously racist." "Racism stares one in the face for it so happens that it belongs in a characteristic whole: that of the shameless exploitation of one group of men by another which has reached a higher stage of technical development. This is why military and economic oppression generally precedes, makes possible, and legitimises racism." (Fanon 1969 pgs. 37-38). Racism cannot be unconscious, cannot be a genetic predisposition for racism is an instrument of power framed, mobilised and operationalised to serve an overall strategy of domination, of exerting hegemony for the generation and extraction of wealth both human and nonhuman. Racism mobilised and operationalised must impact the social order leaving its tell-tale marks on those of the social order and their power relations which demands the strategy to mask the operationalisation of racism in the liberal order of racism of the North Atlantic. This explains the hegemony of black on black racism in the neo-colonial world given the continued existence of an evolved system of exploitation that was birthed by colonial domination.

The Inferiorised

In the text Fanon now deals with the actions of the oppressed in response to the assault of the oppressor as follows: "the racialized social group tries to imitate the oppressor and thereby to deracialise itself. The 'inferior race' denies itself as a different race. It shares with the 'superior race' the convictions, doctrines, and other attitudes concerning it. The oppressor, through the inclusive and frightening character of his authority, manages to impose on the native new ways of seeing, and in particular a pejorative judgment with respect to his original form of existing. This event, which is commonly designated as alienation, is naturally very important. It is found in the official texts under the name of assimilation." (Fanon 1969 pg. 38). The epidermalised, racialized oppressed willingly make themselves objects of power through imitation of the oppressor to deracialise, to de-epidermalise themselves by insisting that they are not a different race, an inferior race for they are white thereby conjuring the contradiction of seeking and insisting on the existence of a condition of being that solely depends of the assent and recognition of massa, the white man, the oppressor. This is then the potent expression of the order of power that the white man wields over those insisting that they are white in their black skins. The oppressed perfect the imitation of white culture and worldviews, including its racism, thereby discarding and redefining what is left of their original ways and worldviews, embracing willingly the hate spewed on them by white discourse condemning themselves to a netherworld where not even the assent of the white man can release them from, for what they insist they are will be vehemently contradicted by their body. Your only choice is then to chemically, cosmetically and surgically alter your body so you bleach your skin, chemically alter your hair, wear Chinese and South Asian hair implants and surgically alter your nose, your eyelids and whatever else in a self-hate driven delusion for your white mind to match a white body. But try as you will and may, you can never be white, such is the power of the white man's hegemony and the futility of our daily existence. This is our reality which we willingly embrace, an alienated existence, which the white man insists to us is assimilation. The conclusion is then obvious, that epidermalisation and deracination with simultaneous racination were tools of racism invented by power to drive us to embrace our alienation willingly, to be content with an alienated existence, to embrace futility for we love assimilation more than life itself. Such is the dynamic of North Atlantic domination/hegemony from the colonial enterprise to the neo-colonial enterprise. Fanon continues on the surrender of the oppressed as follows: "The inferiorised had admitted, since the force of reasoning was implacable, that its misfortunes resulted directly from its racial and cultural characteristics. Guilt and inferiority are the usual consequences of this dialectic. The oppressed then tries to escape these, on the one hand by proclaiming his total and unconditional adoption of the new cultural models, and on the other by proclaiming an irreversible condemnation of his own cultural style." "Having judged, condemned, abandoned his cultural forms, his language, his food habits, his sexual behaviour, his way of sitting down, of resting, of laughing, of enjoying himself, the oppressed flings himself upon the imposed culture with the desperation of a drowning man." (Fanon 1969 pg. 39). Under the weight of the pressure exerted by the order of oppression unleashed by the oppressor, the oppressed bends under the very force of the logic of her/his oppression and embraces the device of guilt postulated by the oppressor's order of power, thereby exonerating the oppressor of all guilt for their imperial enterprise. This guilt that the oppressed wrap themselves in is the necessary precursor to immersion in the desire formulated by the oppressor and operationalised for the oppressor's desire is the premier strategic lynchpin towards having the oppressed make themselves into objects of the oppressor's order of power. Guilt driven by the acceptance and internalisation of inferiority, awakens the desire to be white as the driven snow which embraces white culture, whiteness as a drowning man clutching at straws for all that is non-white and inferior must be rejected, for they are hindrances and stumbling blocks to attain wholeness i.e. whiteness. For before whiteness we were never whole and wholesome that is why we were so easily conquered, which heralds the operational presence of self-immolation, that netherworld where the victim accepts blame for the sins of the white man, thereby exonerating their master race. In such a scenario, this is why in the 21st century the white folks of the North Atlantic refuse to accept that there is a burden to bear and blowback to accept and deal with as a result of their quest for Empire in the world. White folks are then today deeply delusional as they present the symptoms of fear of a black planet which flows from the ravages of their racism on their perceptions.

Racism and the Coloniser

Fanon now deals in the text with racism and the coloniser as follows: "In reality, a colonial country is a racist country. If in England, in Belgium, or in France, despite the democratic principles affirmed by these respective nations, these are still racists, it is these racists who, in their opposition to the country as a whole, are logically consistent. It is not possible to enslave men without logically making them inferior through and through. And racism is only the emotional, affective, sometimes intellectual explanation of this inferiorisation. The racist in a culture with racism is therefore normal. He has achieved a perfect harmony of economic relations and ideology." (Fanon 1967 pgs. 39-40). The legacy of being a colonial country is being a racist country, where being racist is normal, where the democratic principles of these countries simply mask the racist legacy and agenda, for the quest for dominance requires enslavement which is attained only through inferiorisation of the target. Inferiorisation is then applied to all power relations in the quest for hegemony with racism operationalised becoming a manufactured operationalised, explanation of this instrument of power. The racist is as normal as racism in this culture because racism is part of an arsenal of instruments of power utilised to ensure the sustainability of hegemonic discourse and the power relations of the social order, thereby embracing politics and the generation and the distribution of wealth. Racism acts upon the targets of power whilst masking the nature of power through distraction with the fixation on racism, not on power, for power transcends law and there can be no law banishing power, unlike racism. Fanon continues: "And, we repeat, every colonialist group is racist. 'Acculturised' and deculturised at one and at the same time, the oppressed continues to come up against racism. Forgetting racism as a consequence, one concentrates on racism as a cause. Race prejudice in fact obeys a flawless logic. A country that lives, draws its substance from the exploitation of other peoples, makes these people inferior. Race prejudice applied to those people is normal. Racism is therefore not a constant of the human spirit. It is, as we have seen, a disposition fitting into a well-defined system." (Fanon 1969 pgs. 40-41). You cannot be involved in the colonial enterprise and be not racist as you are the recipient of value extracted from the colonised via the hegemonic power relations that constitute the form and nature of the colonial enterprise. These power relations simultaneously deculturise and acculturise the target of the colonial enterprise but the victim of colonial domination fixates on the racism not on the power relations that formulate and operationalise the instrument of racism. This is then the grave strategic mistake where racism is visualised as the cause and strategies are formulated and launched to deal with a causative racism, when in fact racism is a consequence of power relations, ensuring the continuity of the hegemonic colonial power relations into the neo-colonial order as hegemonic power relations thereby ensuring that the grave problematic of the neo-colonial social order is change. For racism is normal and hegemonic under the colonial order and it remains normal, hegemonic and expected under the neo-colonial order but in its black on black racism incarnation, because the power relations that demand the operationalisation of racism were not dismantled with decolonisation.

Racism's Event Horizon

In the text Fanon now states his strategic discourse of vital importance to understanding the threat posed to non-white races in the North Atlantic especially the Arab in the 21st century as follows: "A society has race prejudice or it has not. There are no degrees of prejudice. One cannot say that a given country is racist but that lynchings or extermination camps are not to be found there. The truth is that all that and still other things exist on that horizon. These virtualities, these latencies, circulate, carried by the life-stream of psycho-affective, economic relations." (Fanon pg. 41). In a racist country of the North Atlantic the absence of lynchings and death camps at a given point in its existence does not exclude, banish and guarantee that such expressions/ instruments of racism and state racism are absent from the event horizon of the power relations of the social order. For they are always present, always a possibility to grasp in the politics of a racist North Atlantic country, because the power relations and hegemonic discourse constitutes them as viable and valuable instruments of power, thereby giving them the presence of being operationalised whenever the politics dictate. Racism as an instrument of power will continually place the Final Solution in the political playbook of the North Atlantic and in the 21st century it is the turn of the Arab. Fanon describes the relations that drive this process as the combination of the psycho-affective with the economic, which are aggregated expressions of power relations which pinpoint specific aspects of power relations rather than an expansive description of the operational horizon. Racism is then the consequence of power relations, not its cause, and politics will determine the use of the Final Solution not racism.

State of Grace

Fanon returns to the relationship between the culture abandoned and reembraced by the inferiorised and the pitfalls thereof which result in sterility that ensures the sustainability of the hegemony of the oppressor. Fanon states: "This culture, abandoned, sloughed off, rejected, despised becomes for the inferiorised an object of passionate attachment. There is a very marked kind of overvaluation that is psychologically closely linked to the craving for forgiveness." (Fanon pg. 41). The reembrace of his native culture spurned, hated and dumped is in fact driven by overvaluation for there is no willingness to refurbish, to create a new dynamic to oppose the domination of the oppressor for all the inferiorised is seeking is forgiveness and succour from the assault of the oppressor whilst refusing to walk away from her/his servility to the oppressor. What the inferiorised is in fact doing is manufacturing a revisionist form of native culture in their image and likeness that enables their servility constituting a wounded culture and a wounded civilisation that is at the heart of neo-colonial domination. Fanon continues: "Yet the oppressed goes into ecstasies over each rediscovery. The wonder is permanent. Having formerly emigrated from his culture, the native today explores it with ardour. It is a continual honeymoon. Formerly inferiorised he is now in a state of grace. Not with impunity, however, does one undergo domination. The culture of the enslaved people is sclerosed, dying. No life any longer circulates in it. Or more precisely, the only existing life is dissimulated." (Fanon pgs. 41-42). The inferiorised with her/his reembrace of the native culture is finally in a state of grace, a personal state of grace created to satisfy a personal need which refuses to accept the reality of native culture and cannot mount an intervention towards the regeneration of native culture. The reembrace refuses to accept the reality of domination, especially its impact on the culture that the desire for forgiveness must embrace in its quest for the state of grace. The inferiorised energetically reembraces a dying culture and has no will to reinvigorate this culture, in spite of the much touted love for it, for to do so they must make the ultimate sacrifice which they are not willing to make: to dump the definition and the soul affixed to them, which they earnestly function by and cannot visualise life without it, by the white man. The inferiorised then welcome and systematically function as dictated by the power relations of the oppressor by immersing themselves in the dissimulated life, the life of masks, lies and camouflage and the shucking and jiving of the dying native culture they lustily reembrace, praise and proclaim. For this gives them the best of two worlds: to operate in the world of the oppressor whilst in a state of grace which is also in the world of the oppressor. Those who reembrace are then the fifth columnists of the neo-colonial world. Fanon continues: "the state of grace and aggressiveness are the two constants found at this stage. Aggressiveness being the passion-charged mechanism making it possible to escape the sting of paradox." (Fanon 1969 pg. 42). The state of grace of the inferiorised must generate aggressiveness/aggression both pointing inwards and externally, for there is no liberation from the futility of self-hate and self-immolation within the state of grace as they are seeking relief for the paradoxical condition they have created through aggressiveness. Those encumbered with the state of grace then insist that they represent personally and embody the rebirth of their native culture, which necessitates violence in all its forms against the enemies of this rebirth both within and without the culture. In a state of grace, we have witnessed the evolution of this aggressiveness/aggression expressed as tribal

and ethnic warfare, genocide, military dictators and in the 21st century Salafi-Jihadi Islamic extremism birthed in the neo-colonial world with the North Atlantic as its target. The constants of state of grace and aggressiveness then constitute a racist extremist worldview with those in the state of grace at the centre of the cosmos charged with the fate of mankind. Fanon continues on these constants as follows: "Rediscovering tradition, living it as a defence mechanism, as a symbol of purity, of salvation, the decultured individual leaves the impression that the mediation takes vengeance by substantialising itself. This falling back on archaic positions having no relation to technical development is paradoxical. The institutions thus valorised no longer correspond to the elaborate methods of action already mastered." (Fanon 1969 pg. 42). In this state of grace, the paradox is dominant as the rebirth of tradition is the purity and salvation that the inferiorised desire and more importantly it is the defence they seek but the identified enemies do not present the salient threats for the salient threat is the inferiorised in the state of grace. The inferiorised in the state of grace rails at her/his grave deadly enemies and insist on extremist violence to destroy this threat posed, for the inferiorised in the state of grace enjoy vengeance and hate through the valorisation of institutions they have embraced and defined and the substantialising of the state of grace by insisting that it is the primary and only condition of existence desired and necessary. A condition of existence and reality then exists where the embrace of tradition has no concern for the potency of action and strategy adopted as strategies of action and their discourses already mastered are simply discarded. This is done because the valorised and substantialised traditions and institutions are potently powerful in their purity rendering then unassailable, talismanic. Having them is all you need for vengeance and victory. You are then in the grip of a cycle of rebirth which is framed in apocalyptic terms for it is a selective culling of tradition and rebirth to leave an end product whose definition, strategy and body of strategic action remain the sole preserve of a maximum leader or a small oligarchy. We must then visualise the Khmer Rouge and the Kampuchea enterprise and the Islamic State and the Khilafah enterprise all products of colonial and neo-colonial domination. Fanon continues as follows: "The culture put into capsules, which has vegetated since the foreign domination, is revalorised. It is not reconceived, grasped anew, dynamised from within. It is shouted. And this headlong, unstructured, verbal revalorisation conceals paradoxical attitudes." (Fanon 1969 pg. 42). The culture vegetating under foreign domination is not injected with a new dynamic, a new discourse with new power relations of resistance, but simply appropriated and placed in capsules conceived, defined and bearing the mark of the occupier by the inferiorised. Who then insists that all that is required for the rebirth is to shout out that this is so thereby revalorising a vegetated, dominated culture which can only produce grotesque outcomes for it can never end foreign domination, revitalise native culture nor end the pain of the inferiorised, so the monster created by the surrender to North Atlantic domination embraces the apocalypse and genocide on an industrial scale, enter Pol Pot and the Khmer Rouge and Al Baghdadi and Islamic State. Such is the legacy of North Atlantic domination.

In the text Fanon then presents his position on the response of the occupier to the paradoxical actions of the occupied as follows: "This rediscovery, this absolute valorisation almost in defiance of reality, objectively indefensible, assumes an incomparable and subjective importance. On emerging from these passionate espousals, the native will have decided to fight all forms of exploitation and of alienation of man. At the same time, the occupant, on the other hand, multiplies appeals to assimilation, then to integration, to community." (Fanon 1969 pg. 43). The native wrapped in a paradoxical action plan announces her/his intention to assault the symptoms of the domination of the occupier and in response the occupier replies with an evolving strategy to address the ever present pain of the inferiorised: the unconditional embrace of whiteness from assimilation through to finally community where you will be made whole again. Can the inferiorised resist this strategy of the occupier?

The answer lies in the potency of neo-colonialism in the 21st century. Fanon ends the article by insisting that liberation is possible in spite of the paradoxical reality of the state of grace he potently deconstructed with his final statement illustrating the tension between the need to believe in the possibility of liberation in spite of the insights afforded through analysis. Fanon states: "In conclusion, universality resides in this decision to recognise and accept the reciprocal relativism of different cultures, once the colonial status is irreversibly excluded." (Fanon 1969 pg. 44). But the colonial situation has now been replaced by the neo-colonial situation and the reciprocal relativism of cultures is now mainstream discourse, but the power relations of the neo-colonial world, with especially the USA and the rest of the North Atlantic, illustrate the fact that the dominant/dominated duality prospers and exerts much more impactful power than the occupier/occupied duality ever did, for it has evolved to reflect the changing technological basis of human civilisation and the means to generate wealth. Colonialism died at the necessary juncture in this march of technology and the means to generate wealth, but humanity has not prospered, barbarism is in no way diminished whilst racism remains an instrument of power. Fanon the analyst was then right, for there can be no liberation utilising the state of grace of the inferiorised, and the proof of this is the river of blood that was spilled and continues to be fed across the Third World by the inferiorised in their state of grace, as they continue to serve massa by shedding our blood and offering up our suffering on the altar of the blood lust of the North Atlantic in their quest to be made whole again by those who created them. Smiling, liberal racism is far more potent than massa's racism, as it is the instrument devised by hegemonic power and discourse for this neo-colonial era under the hegemony of austere neoliberal financial markets capitalism.

Chapter 13

In this final chapter of the deconstruction of Fanon's discourse of the Negro and the Arab two articles written by Fanon and published in El Moudjahid in the period 1959-1960 and translated into English and published in "Toward the African Revolution" will be deconstructed.

"Racist Fury in France" published in El Moudjahid in May 1959 deals with the backlash unleashed against Arabs in France as a result of the war for Algerian Independence now using the metropole France as a battlefield, simply the chickens had come home to roost. Fanon states as follows: "spontaneous attitudes of racism and passionate discrimination against North Africans were seen to develop. In an immediate and inclusive way suspicion of the Arabs became second nature. One step was more and the hunt was on." (Fanon 1969 pg. 163). The potent response to the Algerian war for independence now being fought in France was a surge of racist actions against all Arabs, for the problem was not Algerian in origin, but an Arab grave threat to the white homeland.

This is the very said response in the 21st century to the assault of Islamic extremism and then the wave of Arab refugees where in both instances the Final Solution is an inalienable fixture of the event horizon of this singularity. In speaking of the racist events in France Fanon states: "They will show us beyond any doubt that the confusion in the conception of the 'furriner' was not to be attributed to a regrettable ignorance, but had its justification in a principle, a commonplace one, according to which the crudest forms of race discrimination are making headway in France at a truly explosive rate." (Fanon 1969 pg. 164). In response to the Arab threat there is a public expression of a discourse of racism that contradicts the hegemonic discourse of liberal racism.

The lesson here is then apparent, which was again confirmed in the 21st century in the North Atlantic that, when faced with a threat framed by a non-white race the political discourse of racism will now frame and define this threat into an instrument of power to normalise the social order, to mobilise political support to the general and specific benefit of the politicians, to the detriment of the rule of law thereby overdetermining political power in a time of a manufactured national crisis. This political discourse of racism will and continues to give space and impetus to the discourse of "scientific racism," Fascism and National Socialism as it rolls out its action plan to ensure that the 'persistent crisis' is sustainable. In this terrain Fanon points out the reality then of attacks on blacks who are certainly not Arabs, which illustrates the politics of race hate at work in France. Fanon states: "As the perpetrators made no secret of proclaiming, this was a punishment inflicted on the woman (who was white), and a warning administered to the Negro." (Fanon 1969 pg. 164). Racism is at this juncture in France seeking to police and normalise human behaviour contrary to the public discourse of liberal racism. The Arab, the Negro and relations that cross the racial divide are then the targets of normalisation and policing. Fanon then presents the incident at the showing of the anti-racist film in Paris where protests erupted with shouts of "Down with Negroes" "Death to Negroes" and "Long live Hitler." Fanon states: "When it is possible in France for an anti-racist film to be attacked in broad daylight by an organisation that does not fear to proclaim the slogan, 'Death to Negroes!' it can be said that democracy in France is in a bad way and that Negroes would do well to leave the ship." (Fanon 1969 pg. 165). Fanon is now showing his talents as a political agitator as he is now insisting that it is now time for the Negroes to leave France given the perilous racist attacks. What is again apparent is the continuity between France in the late 1950s and the North Atlantic in the 21st century, the commonality is the threat posed by the enemy non-white races as these are the gravest threats, with the latest addition to this being the Slavs of Russia which completes the list that beckons to the Final Solution. On the origin of this wave of racism expressed publicly and politically in France in the late 1950s Fanon states as follows: "These manifestations spring straight from the heart, that is to say from the heart of the individual, express both the vice of French education with reference to the rest of humanity, and decades of colonial domination." (Fanon 1969 pg. 166). Fanon is insisting that a repository of racism exists in the French individual, deposited and protected by the French education structure and the legacy of colonial domination. Fanon ends his article with a statement that is of grave relevance in the second decade of the 21st century in the North Atlantic as follows: "It is up to the members of the 'French Community' to decide whether their place is still by the side of those who have not rid themselves either of indignities or of hatred toward the black race." (Fanon 1969 pg. 166).

The majority white race of the North Atlantic has then to choose the path they will adopt concerning racism and the use of racism as an instrument of power to normalise the North Atlantic social order. The abiding lesson of this Fanon article in 1959 is the cyclical nature of use of the political discourse of racism in the North Atlantic to the benefit of the political elites and the oligarchy they serve. In the first and second decade of the 21st century the political discourse is evolving and increasingly embracing public and political expressions of racism framed in a discourse of political racist extremism.

The next article was published in El Moudjahid in 1960 and translated into English and published in "Toward the African Revolution" as "Blood Flows in the Antilles under French Domination." In this article Fanon deals with unrest in Fort-de-France, Martinique and the manner in which it was suppressed by the French military within the context of Martinique being an overseas department of France not a colony. In December 1959 riots between the black population and the French state broke out with the application of grave state power to return the blacks to their place in the social order and to end the challenge the rioters posed to white hegemony. Fanon states: "Those ornaments of the empire, those castrated countries that gave such good and loyal servants are beginning to stir. The West Indians, once was told on all sides, are French, like the Corsicans. And these enormous masses of West Indians, men and women who believed in it. Yet despite this great intoxication, despite this enormous imposture, there were Martinicans who entered into open struggle against the French forces," (Fanon 1969 pg. 167). In spite of the assault upon the black population of Martinique from colonial domination to being an overseas department of France; contrary to the docility of the black population through these historical periods illustrated by their embrace of the discourse of assimilation, of being French, in December 1959 riots erupted in Fort-de-France. The liberal racist veneer in December 1959 was simply scraped away. Fanon continues: "In reality the problem has been raised. And this is all to the good. The fiction of the French Antilles, the formula is now again challenged. And this is all to the good." (Fanon 1969 pg. 168). The December 1959 riots then placed on the political agenda the problematic that drives the French Antilles and the discourse of assimilation. This problematic is then created by the continued operationalisation of racism as an instrument of power in the French Antilles, and this generates not only servility but resistance of an explosive nature as it is the response triggered to a gnawing, daily abrasiveness of racial discrimination in a department of France with a black majority. The white response is the sustainable underdevelopment of the Caribbean overseas departments, where the potential for black resistance and rebellion will be literally contained and framed by deprivation, which is a strategy of punishing those with a white perceived penchant for resistance and revolt. The failure of this strategy in French Guiana is potently illustrated by the operational strength of transnational organised crime in this overseas department, where they thrive utilising the links to Europe whilst fully exploiting the chronically underdeveloped state and the emaciated structure of wealth creation which is still in the colonial era. Fanon continues: "The old politicians, assimilated, harassed from within, must today be very worried. They are also discovering the existence of a rebellious spirit, of a national spirit." "At this time, the French forces and their allies, the present politicians, deputies, and senators will undoubtedly break this first manifestation of the national spirit of Martinique. But we know now that the people of Guadeloupe, of Martinique, and of Guiana will be independent and will build their respective countries as they see fit." (Fanon 1969 pg. 169). Fanon recognises that the rebellion of Martinique will be defeated but going back to his idyllic, he insists that there will be independence for the three overseas departments of France in the Caribbean which is presently a dead issue in the politics of the three overseas departments. The 2017 protests in French Guiana illustrate this reality as there was no call from this protest movement for independence, what was demanded was an improved wealth generation system that raised the standard of living and a refurbished state to deal with social issues expressed via an accord with the state to spend more in French Guiana. The strategy of containment via underdevelopment married to racism is then successful to date. Looking past Fanon's idyllic, the potency of his discursive concepts to deconstruct the reality of the Caribbean is once again painfully obvious, especially for those with a linear concept of freedom and its attainability.

These two articles present continuities of Fanon's discourse of racism and culture thereby affirming the potency of his deconstruction of the discourses of racism of the North Atlantic. This potency establishes the operational certainty that Fanon's discourse is then the foundation upon which to build the discourse of liberation of the Caribbean. This is not a foundation premised on orthodox dogmatism but a recognition that it commences with Fanon's discourse, which drives the task of review and the creation of new discourse to ensure that the process of liberation is always situated in real time relevance. Fanon's embrace of his idyllic, his profound belief that the Revolution was inevitable is the gravest weakness of his discourse, which he addressed in the final text of his oeuvre "The Wretched of the Earth", which must be wrestled with in my time and in the future and the key to this engagement is the focus on power, power relations and resistance.

Conclusion

This deconstruction of Fanon's discourse of racism and culture, the Negro and the Arab exposes the task at hand of working within the confines of North Atlantic discourse whilst undertaking the quest for liberation from North Atlantic domination. The conclusion is inescapable from Fanon's discourse that there is no liberation to be grasped whilst seeking liberation within the confines of North Atlantic discourse. Fanon's texts deconstructed in this work establishes the frailty and plain irrelevance of specific North Atlantic discourses to understand and explain our reality towards liberation and Fanon presents alternative methods of interpretation and a worldview but the taint of North Atlantic discourse exists, and its impact on Fanon's worldview is apparent. Fanon gestures towards the need to walk away from feeble, racist North Atlantic discourse but in the works deconstructed in this text especially "Black Skin White Masks" he remains trapped in a North Atlantic enlightenment discourse which he modified, seen in his attitude to Hegel, the dialectic and Historical Materialism. It is from historical materialism and his embrace of the dialectic Fanon frames his idyllic of the Revolution and the certainty of its realisation, without due regard to the dynamic of power relations and the power to subvert a quest for Revolution. This idyllic appears in Fanon's text at times in contradiction to the flow of the analysis he was undertaking, which was potently indicating the problematic of Revolution in the daily life of the oppressed and the inferiorised. At given times in the flow of the analysis of the text Fanon's insistence that Revolution is inevitable appears as imposingly necessary, for without Revolution there is no validation of, or possibility of resistance, making racist domination inevitable giving the impression that Fanon had to be convinced that the inferiorised, especially of the West Indian variety, can make a Revolution. This juxtaposition gives the impression of a Fanon in denial, seeking to escape his analytic outcomes, which is the product of Fanon's embrace of the discourse of revolution formulated by the adherents of historical materialism with all its grave flaws. What cannot be denied is the recurring and widening fault lines in his works studied in this text where his analytical skills were placing grave and potent pressures on his discourse, worldview and methodology. Fanon in this period was then in the turmoil of a discursive break which resulted in an ongoing process of personal debate and resolution as illustrated by the changes in his two books that followed especially in "The Wretched of the Earth." What is now necessary is to extend and complete the discursive break much more in depth than the position Fanon reached in "The Wretched of the Earth" by utilising Fanon's analytical tools, purged of its enlightenment pollutants. When this purge is affected his legacy becomes starkly apparent, especially his advances pointing to the formulation of a new knowledge as follows: the refusal to theorise married to the use of reality uncovered by the analyses of power relations to falsify and debunk white knowledges, the analysis of power relations as the primary focus of his work, the formulation of a discourse of total liberation and most importantly the combination of analyses of power relations with personal political action. Fanon's legacy must then be immersed within an anti-enlightenment discourse and welded together with an emphasis on, and analysis of power, power/force relations and resistance. These analytic tools, methodology and outcomes are then the basis of Fanon's legacy to us to be preserved, critiqued and built upon to ensure time/space relevance. We must then jettison all North Atlantic enlightenment discourse, reject the Enlightenment by seeing what it is exactly. We must reject historical materialism as it is part of North Atlantic enlightenment discourse, no different from the others. You simply cannot view Fanon's legacy through enlightenment spectacles and find the potency of this legacy, for they are mutually irreconcilable. Finally, the task of formulating knowledge must be separated by dint of the terrain to which it will be applied, for the reality of the Caribbean is not that of Europe and the USA. When building knowledge of the Caribbean, Fanon is the foundation upon which we build, for all knowledge that insists it is Caribbean knowledge must be deconstructed by Fanon's discourse and worldview to ascertain its efficacy.

Visit my website to browse my list of books and articles at: https://www.daurius.com

References

Fanon, Frantz (1977): "Black Skin, White Masks" Grove Press Inc. USA

Fanon, Frantz (1969): "Toward the African Revolution" Grove Press Inc. USA

Also by Daurius Figueira

Discourse of Slavery

Massa's White Supremacist Discourse of West Indian Negro Slavery
Deconstructed Volume 1
Massa's White Supremacist Discourse of West Indian Negro Slavery
Deconstructed Volume 2

Frantz Fanon for the 21st Century

Frantz Fanon for the 21st Century Volume 1 Frantz Fanon's Discourse of
Racism and Culture, the Negro and the Arab Deconstructed
Frantz Fanon for the 21st Century Volume 2 Frantz Fanon's Discourse of
Decolonisation and Violence, the Nature of Power and Power Relations of
Neo-colonial African States,
Frantz Fanon for the 21st Century Volume 3 The Algerian Revolution, Islamic
Discourse, the Colonizer and the Discourse of White Supremacy

Standalone

Belize: Human Smuggling, Transnational Organised Crime, Politicians And
Public Servants
Biopower, Racism, State Racism and The Modern/Post Modern North
Atlantic State: Michel Foucault's Genealogy of the Historico-Political
Discourse of Race War Deconstructed

Derek Walcott's Poetry Deconstructed, Its Political and Sociological Discourse Revealed

Transnational Organized Crime and Drug Trafficking in the Second Decade of the 21st Century in the Dominican Republic, Suriname, Venezuela, French Guiana, Martinique and Guadeloupe

The Islamic State and the Muslims of Trinidad and Tobago in the 21st Century

A Deconstruction of Michel Foucault's 1979 Discourse of Neo-Liberalism for the 21st Century

A Deconstruction of Qu'ranic Discourse for the 21st Century

Watch for more at https://www.daurius.com.

About the Author

Daurius Figueira is a researcher, analyst and author located in the anti-Enlightenment and anti-Science discourse/worldview/paradigm specialising in the study of the illicit drug trade, the illicit small arms trade and human smuggling of the Caribbean, Islamic extremism and racism/white supremacy with an emphasis on power relations. You can access his website to experience and download his research papers published online and view his range of books. His website address is: https://www.daurius.com and his blog on the Caribbean is at: https://drugtrade.wordpress.com/

Read more at https://www.daurius.com.

9 789769 678798